C000049525

HOW TO

(HAVE FUN)

AND NOT DIE!

By Kyle Ashton

Dedicated to my loveable sister, who never says no to an adventure.

To my dad and grandpa who helped teach me how to ski,

And to everyone who bought my first book

How to Snowboard (Have Fun) and Not Die.

The support you've all shown inspires me to keep writing.

CONTENTS

PROLOGUE

Skiing is unlike any other sport. Instead of competing with other teams or athletes, most skiers will find success by reaching individual goals or milestones. Skiing is a sport where concepts like "winning" or "losing" tend to lose their significance. The sensations of speed, a rapid descent, and the frictionless movement is something that is hard to understand by those who haven't experienced it. Strapping on a pair of skis comes with the expectation of being thrilled. Skiing is immensely rewarding, regardless of the skier's skill level. Learning how to ski is a remarkable feeling, and once the concept becomes intuitive the mountain becomes yours to conquer.

The goal of this book is to make skiing accessible to everyone, so that anyone can experience the joys of this sport. The concepts I teach are essentially the same concepts that you'd be taught in a private lesson from ski instructors. With over two decades of skiing and snowboarding experience as both a ski and snowboard instructor, I have taught hundreds (if not thousands) of students the fundamentals needed to safely, comfortably, and efficiently progress their abilities in these sports. Over the years, I discovered an effective process that expedites learning and heightens a person's understanding of these winter sports. Whether you've never seen the snow before, or you just want to brush up on some lessons before hitting the slopes, this book holds the insight you'll need to succeed as a skier. With the information this book provides at your disposal, you will have everything you need to thrive while safely practicing this difficult sport.

Make no mistake, skiing is a difficult sport to master. However, mastery shouldn't be your goal. At the end of the day, skiing is supposed to be a fun activity. Where other sports have clear winners and losers, the winners on a ski slope are the people enjoying themselves. Instead of competing with other athletes, a skier's competition can only be found by looking in the mirror. The challenge of skiing is overcoming your own fears and utilizing what you've learned until it becomes internalized as muscle memory. Knowing that you've challenged yourself to try something new makes skiing a worthwhile endeavor. You're free to progress at your own pace and enjoy every moment.

Even at the highest levels in this sport, professional skiers are encouraged to do what they love (which is skiing). That's why this book aims to teach skiing in a way that is as easy as it is fun. If I've done my job correctly you'll be able to improve your capabilities in this sport, enjoy your experience, stay safe while practicing, and understand how to utilize fundamental techniques to improve over time. Not only does this book cover the standard lesson progression that turns beginners into experts, it is also a comprehensive guide to skiing. That means we'll cover additional topics like ski equipment and the potential hazards that a skier might encounter. Nobody has fun when they are injured or improperly equipped for the conditions, so it's important to understand the potential risks in this frigid environment.

How to Ski (Have Fun) and Not Die! is your guide to learning how to ski in a safe, entertaining, and effective manner. Whether you are interested in becoming a downhill skier, cross-country explorer, or a terrain park terror, I'll show you how to make the most of your time on the mountain. Now let's get started!

1 TERMINOLOGY

Before we get too ahead of ourselves, we should cover some unique terms used by skiers to communicate various concepts. These established terms may be unfamiliar, so it will be beneficial to learn this terminology in order to communicate with other riders. In the following chapters, I will frequently use some of these terms to teach certain concepts. If you find a word or phrase in this book that you're unfamiliar with later on, it might be one of the terms listed here.

All-mountain *(noun):*

Refers to everything the mountain has to offer, including all types of terrain and snow conditions (expert terrain, beginner terrain, fresh powder, compact snow, ice, etc.).

"I thought about using specialized powder skis today, but my all-mountain skis perform so well in all conditions. I'm

so used to the reliability they provide that it's hard to justify using anything else!"

Backcountry *(noun):*

The out-of-bounds sections bordering a ski resort, or ski terrain that is not associated with a ski resort.

"I like going into the backcountry sections near ski resorts, but I'd really enjoy booking a helicopter tour to access Alaska's legendary backcountry terrain."

Base *(noun):*

The bottom of a ski, which is the area that touches the snow when a skier is standing.

"I accidentally skied over those exposed rocks. Now my bases are all scratched up!"

Carving *(verb):*

An advanced type of turn where a skier balances on their edges. Carving requires enough momentum to hold deep turns, which puts a skier's body more horizontal than usual.

"You need some more speed to start carving turns like me!"

Catching an edge *(verb phrase):*

A common mistake that can occur while skiing. "Catching an edge" is what happens when a ski's edge sticks into the snow, which throws the skier off balance. While the bottom of skis are flat, the metal edge that borders each ski are sharp and can carve into snow or ice. When improperly utilized, these edges can "catch" the snow. Catching an edge will generally lead to a crash.

"I angled my skis the wrong way and caught an edge, which threw me off balance. Luckily the snow was forgiving, so I corrected the angle of my skis and managed to avoid crashing."

Clipping in *(verb):*

The act of attaching your ski's bindings to the ski boot itself. Because attaching your skis requires a skier to step on their binding, it is also referred to as "stepping in." It can also be called "strapping in," although strapping in is more closely associated with snowboard bindings or the act of tightening of your ski boots. These terms are interchangeable when it comes to attaching your skis.

"Are you finished clipping into your skis? I already strapped up my ski boots. Let's step in and go already!"

Fall line *(noun):*

The fall line is the direction of travel a slope naturally takes. If you were to take a ball and let it roll down the mountain, it would follow a predictable path. This path is known as the fall line, and it is also the path of least resistance. Skiers generally follow the fall line when skiing, but can also change their course if needed.

"If we follow the fall line the path goes straight to the chairlifts. We could also traverse horizontally, avoiding the fall line, to head back towards the ski lodge."

Grind *(verb):*

The act of skiing on a surface that isn't snow. Grinding on skis typically involves rails, boxes, or similar smooth surfaces. Most of these features can be found in terrain parks or while skiing in urban environments.

"Did you see me grind that metal rail in the terrain park?"

Groomers *(noun):*

The groomed runs at a ski resort, sometimes called "groomers," are trails that have been smoothed over to create a compacted and uniformly flattened ski run.

Groomed snow offers a reliable surface to practice on, especially when snow conditions are not ideal.

"The ground is getting icy and everything else is getting tracked out. Let's go back to the groomed runs, where the snow conditions are more predictable."

Lift *(noun):*

An abbreviated word for "chairlift." Lifts can also refer to other lift systems like pomas, rope tows, gondolas, etc. In other words, a lift refers to the thing that you're using to reach the top of a ski run.

"If we get separated, meet me at the main lift!"

Muscle memory *(noun):*

The ability to reproduce movement like it is second nature, almost instinctively. Muscle memory is developed through repetitive motion.

"Ever try brushing your teeth with your other hand? It's much harder because your other hand doesn't have the muscle memory to effortlessly make those small muscle movements. I'm going to practice skiing until my muscle memory is so strong that I could ski blindfolded! Not that I would do that, of course."

Nose *(noun):*

The leading or front-facing tips of the skis are called the nose-end. The nose-end is where your toe points to when attached to the ski.

"The noses of my skis dug into the snow, which caused me to crash. What a mess!"

Pitch *(noun):*

Refers to the angle or slope of a ski run.

"The pitch of this run is fairly steep. We should practice on a safer slope until snow conditions improve."

Powder *(noun):*

Refers to snowfall that is fresh, dry, and/or deep.

"The powder is good today! Yesterday's snow was pretty dense, but today the powder is light and fluffy."

Riders *(noun):*

The general catch-all term for snow sport enthusiasts is "riders." While skiing is probably the most recognizable downhill snow sport, there are many emerging snow sports (such as snow skates and snow bikes). Instead of referring to other people as snow skiers or snowboarders, you can just call them riders.

"There are a lot of other riders on the ski slope today. I saw snowboarders, skiers, and a few homemade snow skates. I even saw a rider getting on the chairlift with a snow tricycle, which looks like a lot of fun!"

Run *(noun):*

Sections of a hill are divided into different runs. Different runs usually have unique names based on specific landmarks or features. Runs at ski resorts are labeled with a difficulty rating, such as blue squares for intermediate-level trails or green circles for gentler slopes.

"This run is an intermediate-level trail called 'Little Trees,' and it has lots of little trees we need to avoid. Be sure and stay to the right or you'll end up at 'Cliffhanger,' which is a double-black diamond expert-level run we're probably not ready for."

Shred *(verb):*

The act of skiing, snowboarding, or riding in the snow. Shredding the slopes is just another way of saying you're skiing the mountain, although it's not exclusive to skiing.

"You've got your snowboard and I've got my skis. Now let's shred this powder!"

Switch *(adverb):*

Riding switch is when someone is skiing backwards. A skier riding switch will have their back facing downhill instead of their chest. Riding switch is an advanced technique, and it's best to practice this on shallow slopes before attempting to ride switch on steeper terrain.

"Did you see Caroline land that jump switch? That was incredible!"

Tail *(noun):*

Refers to the back-end of a ski, which is located behind a skier's heel.

"Did you see how much snow I was flinging off my tails?"

Top sheet *(noun):*

The top of a ski, opposite of a ski's base.

"Don't worry about scratching your top sheet. I know the design looks cool, but damaging your top sheet doesn't affect your skiing. Scratching your base though? Now that's another story."

Tracked out *(verb phrase):*

Tracked out snow, sometimes called chopped up snow, is a type of snow condition created by skiers and other riders. Riding in fresh snow leaves distinctive tracks in the snow, while simultaneously compacting or shifting the snow underfoot. These tracks accumulate, creating the snow conditions that are referred to as "tracked out snow." When the snow becomes tracked out it becomes less desirable for a number of reasons, which is something we'll discuss more in later chapters. Tracked out snow can also expose ice or rocks, which creates more dangerous snow conditions for skiers.

"This section of the hill is tracked out and a sheet of ice has been exposed underneath the snow. It's becoming more

dangerous to ski here, so we should find a new run to practice on."

Wipeout *(noun):*

Another way to refer to a crash on your skis.

"I shouldn't have hit that jump. It was a total wipeout!"

Yard sale *(noun):*

The more extreme version of a wipeout is what's known as a "yard sale." This is a crash that removes equipment, leaving gear strewn around the mountain. You'll often see skiers walking uphill to retrieve their ski poles after a yard sale.

"That was one of the worst yard sales I've ever had. I lost my ski poles, goggles, skis, and even a glove! What a crash! Can you help me find my headphones?"

2 RULES OF THE ROAD

When skiing at a resort you'll be sharing the slopes with other riders. Much like driving on the road, there are some basic rules that everyone must follow in order to prevent collisions and stay safe.

Etiquette on the mountain should come naturally to most people, as a little common sense and courtesy for others is all it takes to avoid potential accidents with other people. New skiers should familiarize themselves with the rider guidelines, as following these rules helps ensure your safety and the safety of the riders around you. These simple guidelines are recognized worldwide, so memorize them and take them to heart.

Rider Guidelines:

Riders Ahead of You Have the Right of Way

This is a rule that most people instinctively understand, because we all recognize the fact that other people don't have eyes in the back of their head. People ahead of you who are actively skiing downhill aren't able to react when approached from behind. If a person collides with someone downhill from them, it's likely due to a lack of control or a complete disregard for others. That's why people downslope of you have the right-of-way.

Be aware that the riders downhill from you can change direction. Sometimes there will be people downhill from you who suddenly turn or start traversing sideways, so give other riders plenty of room when passing them. Just because someone is a faster skier doesn't mean they are suddenly entitled to the entire mountain, so if you see someone taking unnecessary risks around other riders feel free to alert ski patrol.

With that being said, it's worth noting that you should be aware of the general flow of traffic on the mountain. People on a ski slope generally follow the fall line of a slope, which is the path of least resistance down a mountain. While the people uphill from you are expected to yield, moving against the flow of traffic makes your actions harder to anticipate and can cause accidents. For reference, imagine you're driving behind a car that is constantly switching lanes or turning into oncoming traffic. While other drivers (or in this case riders) will do their best to avoid a collision, there is a certain level of expectation to follow the flow of traffic on the mountain. Going against the normal flow of traffic or traversing across the mountain laterally can put you at a higher risk of colliding with other riders.

The best practice is to anticipate the normal flow of skiing traffic, while simultaneously yielding to the riders downhill from you. As a beginner though, you shouldn't worry too much about what the riders behind you are doing. Your attention should be focused on the riders or obstacles ahead of you.

STOPPING UNDER A JUMP OR BLOCKING THE TRAILS IS PROHIBITED

Normally a person downhill from you has the right of way, however, there are certain sections of the mountain that are too dangerous to occupy. This is because other riders cannot see a person who is standing underneath a steep drop or a jump. Intelligent people will send someone ahead to spot their landings below a jump or cautiously check blind spots in order to prevent potential collisions, but this isn't always possible if a person is riding alone. That's why you should never stand below a jump or a steep drop. Uphill riders simply won't see you in these areas, which creates a situation where you could be hit.

Blocking the trails is another instance where other riders may have difficulty avoiding a collision, especially if the trail is narrow or funnels into a choke point. Stopping in congested areas or after a sharp turn is a recipe for disaster, so only stop or take breaks in wide-open areas where other people can see you from a distance.

If you do end up crashing or accidentally stopping in a section where other riders cannot see you, do your best to move quickly away from the danger zone. Ski or walk to a location with more visibility, where uphill riders can clearly see you. If nothing else, travel to the sides of a ski run. Generally speaking, the sides of a ski slope have less traffic from other riders.

CONTROL YOURSELF AT ALL TIMES

If you find yourself struggling to control your skis, it likely means that you are practicing on a slope that is too steep for your current ability level. There's no shame in finding a less extreme slope to work on your fundamentals, which should give you more control over your skis. It's important to maintain control at all times, because losing control can quickly lead to a potentially dangerous crash.

Once you've learned the fundamental skiing techniques and are practicing on a hill within your current ability level, you'll find it's much easier to control your skis at all times. We'll discuss how to achieve greater control over your skis in later chapters, specifically in the chapter about lesson progression.

LOOK UPHILL AND YIELD TO OTHERS WHEN MERGING TRAILS

While downhill riders may have the right of way, you'll still need to be aware of the riders uphill from you when merging trails. Similar to merging onto the freeway while driving, merging trails while skiing creates a situation where riders traveling at high speeds converge (and potentially collide). You can think of the uphill trail as the "freeway" in this situation, and the merging trail must slow down or yield to traffic. Similar to freeways, other riders will generally give the intersection some room to merge safely. It's also a good habit to slow down when approaching an intersection, regardless of whether you are the uphill or downhill rider.

READ ALL WARNING SIGNS AND AVOID CLOSED SECTIONS OR FEATURES

Reading the posted warning signs at a ski area helps keep riders updated on specific hazards that are subject to change (due to changing conditions, weather, etc.). For example, there are rocks or trees that may only be exposed when the snow coverage is sparse or after experiencing snowmelt. Most ski resorts are aware of specific dangers that appear when conditions are right, and ski patrol generally does a good job of closing these areas or posting warning signs. Reading the signage posted throughout the resort will help you stay informed about the potential dangers in the area and helps riders navigate the trails safely.

OUT-OF-BOUNDS IS NOT PATROLLED, ENTER AT OWN RISK OR PERIL

Out-of-bounds areas are not monitored by ski patrol, which means that hazards are not marked and you won't be easily found if you get into trouble. While it's possible to find great skiing spots in these areas, there are risks to consider if you ski out-of-bounds.

If you are skiing outside of a ski resort or in the out-of-bounds regions near a ski resort, it is very important to exercise caution. It's a good idea to use an experienced guide and to utilize all the safety equipment you possibly can. When skiing out of bounds you should ski in groups so that one rider can cautiously approach low-visibility areas for a closer inspection. If the terrain passes inspection, the rest of the group should be able to safely descend. Skiing in groups is also beneficial if any accidents were to occur.

I recommend avoiding out-of-bounds areas, especially when you're still learning the fundamentals of skiing. While it can be exciting to explore untouched terrain, the risks far outweigh the rewards. Even skiers with a tremendous level of expertise and preparation can easily get into trouble while skiing out-of-bounds. Think twice before you start ducking into places that ski resorts can't reliably maintain or patrol.

ALERT SKI PATROL IF YOU SEE AN ACCIDENT, UNMARKED HAZARDS, OR DANGEROUS ACTIVITY

Repeat violators of the rider guidelines put themselves and others at risk, which is why most reputable ski resorts take safety seriously and will revoke the lift tickets of dangerous riders. It's also the job of ski patrol to respond to injuries that require their attention. Be sure to alert ski patrol if you witness an accident, discover unmarked hazards, or observe potentially dangerous activity.

I also recommend having a safety plan in place for yourself and your riding group. This safety plan would include things like carrying safety equipment, staying within communication range (for example by using something like a long-distance walkie-talkie), and agreeing to a meeting place if anyone in your riding group becomes lost or separated.

Similar to an airplane, where securing your own air mask is recommended before assisting others, you must think about your own safety on the mountain to ensure the safety of the riders around you. These simple guidelines will help keep you safe and, by extension, protect the other riders around you. Follow these rules to ensure that everyone can share the mountain, avoid collisions, and have fun.

3 EQUIPMENT GUIDE

Before we talk about how to ski, let's discuss the equipment skiers use to flourish in frigid climates. The goal of this chapter isn't to showcase top-of-the-line gear, although we will talk about what makes certain equipment more suited to your specific needs. The primary goal of this chapter is to educate new skiers about the protective equipment that's necessary to conquer the arctic elements that skiers will experience.

Unlike athletes participating in more conventional sports, skiers can encounter some of the harshest weather conditions imaginable. Skiers that are unprepared for these cold climate extremes could easily have a miserable experience. Skiing can also be outright dangerous without adequate protective gear to prevent potentially life-threatening conditions like frostbite or hypothermia. I can't tell you how many times I've taught lessons to students who were wearing cotton sweatshirts and jeans, and it shouldn't surprise you to learn that these are the students who never returned for a second lesson.

Fortunately, I've organized a handy-dandy gear checklist for you to gather the necessary equipment. Having the right gear can make a significant difference in how you experience and appreciate this sport. Without further ado, let's cover the specialized equipment you'll need as a skier in order to protect yourself from the elements and enjoy this sport to the fullest.

THE SKIS

As odd as it sounds, I would argue that skis are perhaps the least important pieces of equipment you'll need in order to enjoy your time on the mountain. I'd adamantly insist that snow gloves, an insulated snow jacket, and the proper pair of snow pants are much more important for beginners just learning how to enjoy the sport. That being said, it's very hard to practice skiing without skis, although not entirely impossible (as icy sidewalks can attest).

Since skis are generally the first pieces of equipment people will think about when it comes to skiing, let's discuss what makes skis different and why some skis might be a better choice for your goals compared to others.

There are eight variables that determine how different models of skis perform: length, width, ski shape (camber/rocker/flat), tail shape, rigidity, material used, weight, and edge shape. Although all skis will generally behave the same way, the differences in these variables can help some skis perform better than others in specific conditions. Choosing the right ski will depend on the type of skiing you want to do.

The **length** of your ski can dynamically change the performance of a ski. Longer skis offer more stability at high speeds, are more forgiving to balance on at low speeds, can help skiers bust through cruddy snow, and generally float well in powder. However, long skis can be challenging for beginners due to their limited turning capabilities. Shorter skis are generally lighter, easier to maneuver, and respond quickly to turns once initiated.

That said, shorter skis can also be challenging for beginners due to their limited stability and restricted all-mountain utility.

As a general rule, your recommended ski length is the same as the height between your upper chest area and the bottom of your chin. The recommended ski length will change depending on things like height, weight, and the type of skiing you're doing. For example, slightly longer skis might provide stability for someone who is much heavier or taller than average. Long skis are sometimes preferred by skiers interested in off-trail exploration or downhill racing, while shorter skis are sometimes favored by people performing tricks or practicing the fundamentals of skiing.

Ski **width** is another important factor, and wide skis are a relatively recent innovation in this sport. The most noticeable difference you'll notice about wider skis is how easily they float in deep snow. Wide skis excel at rising to the snow's surface and effortlessly staying on top of fresh powder. They are favored by veterans of this sport who prefer to ski in fresh snow for this exact reason.

There are some downsides to having wider skis though. Notably, the added surface area can put greater strain on a skier's knee ligaments. They also tend to be heavier, which can make them unwieldy in certain conditions. Beginners should probably avoid learning on skis with excessive width, as beginners generally learn how to ski on compact snow instead of deep powder. If you experience uncomfortable pressure on your knees while skiing, you'll likely want to consider using smaller, slimmer, or lighter skis.

Rocker is a term that describes a ski's shape, specifically the slight "U-shape" that is reminiscent of a rocking chair. A ski with rocker would feel bendy, flexible, and playful underfoot. Skis with rockers are advantageous for skiers who are mostly interested in performing tricks or prefer the unique feel of a rockered ski. Rockered skis also tend to do well in fresh snow, due to their shape that helps a ski rise to the surface. However, some skiers will find rockers unreliable in situations that require stability and reliability, such as steep terrain, high-speed skiing, and unpredictable snow conditions.

Camber is the exact opposite ski shape of a rocker, where the "U-shape" is flipped upside down like an arch. As you can probably assume, this offers a much different skiing experience compared to other ski shapes. Cambered skis provide distinct contact points in the snow that results in reliable turn initiation, and while they are less playful underfoot they are also less "squirrely." Stability, easy handling, stronger carving, and responsive turning are the highlights of skis with a cambered shape. The downside is that they can be easier to catch an edge with, which could throw your balance off and cause a crash. Cambered skis also lack the "springy" feel that skis with rockers have, although that's a small price to pay for their overall reliability and performance. While a ski with camber will perform exceptionally well in compact snow or ice, their shape has a tendency to sink in deep powder. That being said, it's possible to compensate for this sinking effect by leaning further back towards the tail-ends of your skis in deep snow.

To make things more confusing, many skis are designed with both cambered and rockered sections to get the best of both worlds. These skis generally offer a good balance between the two ski shapes, but you should be aware of how the placement of the cambers or rockers will impact the overall performance. Pay attention to where the ski's binding is located on these types of skis, as the binding placement can give you some idea of how the combination of cambers and rockers will behave on the snow.

Flat skis are another ski shape to consider, although this ski shape is fairly self-explanatory compared to previous ski shapes. Flat skis are also becoming harder to find, which means you probably won't see any of these outside of a garage sale or a ski swap event. While many skis have flat areas in their design, purely flat skis are an outdated ski shape that lack the exceptional performance of a cambered or rockered ski. Flat skis can be a decent starter ski for beginners, however, the innovative ski shapes that newer skis offer has made the flat ski all but obsolete. Flat skis lack the carving and edge control of a cambered ski, yet they also lack the playful feel of a rockered ski.

In addition to the overall shape of a ski, a ski's **tip shape** can differ depending on the intended use. Practically all modern skis utilize a curled front tip, which prevents the nose of the skis from digging into the snow and helps a skier stay on top of deep snow. Twin-tip skis are curled on both the nose and tail, which is beneficial for skiers who intend to ride backwards or land jumps in switch position. If the tail-ends of a ski are not curled, they are called directional skis. Directional skis are designed to travel forwards, whereas twin-tip skis are designed to travel forwards and backwards.

The **rigidity** of a ski refers to its flexibility or "bendiness." The rigidity of a ski can be influenced by the shape, such as the case with a rockered ski. The material used to make a pair of skis can also impact the rigidity.

Flexible skis can be fun to use, especially for skiers with a "loosey-goosey" style. Flexible skis might also be beneficial for skiers looking for a little extra impact absorption when landing jumps. However, flexible skis don't offer the same stability that more rigid skis offer in unfavorable snow conditions or when moving at high speeds. Flexible skis can also experience what is known as "chatter," which is an excessive vibration that reverberates through the skis at high speeds or through bumps. Chatter is somewhat comparable to the "speed wobbles" that skateboarders and longboarders can experience, where the ability to control oneself can suddenly become restricted. Rigidity or flexibility can significantly impact how a ski performs, and your preferred flexibility will depend on the type of skiing you intend to do.

The **materials** a manufacturer uses to build their skis can contribute to the ski's weight, rigidity, and lasting durability. In some cases, a manufacturer might build their skis using cheap materials to cut costs and reduce overhead. An extreme example of this would be a manufacturer who uses plastic to line the edges of a ski, instead of the standard metal edges that can be tuned or sharpened over time. A ski that uses plastic edges would degrade quickly and perform poorly when compared to skis with a metal edge. I should add a disclaimer here that I've never actually seen a ski that uses plastic edges, I'm just using this example to highlight my point. Since skis are an expensive purchase, you should pay attention to the materials a ski manufacturer uses to ensure that you're getting a quality product. Most manufacturers do a good job of detailing the materials a ski uses, why they are being used, and the effects that these materials have on the ski.

The **weight** of a ski will depend on the materials used and the overall size of the ski. Heavier skis can help a skier bust through cruddy snow, are resistant to changes in speed, and reduce or eliminate the vibrations that lighter or more flexible skis can experience. The downside is that heavy skis are clunky, less maneuverable, and more resistant to turning. Skiers looking to perform tricks or hit jumps will tend to prefer lighter skis, while extreme downhill skiers tend to gravitate towards slightly sturdier (and thus heavier) skis. Since you can find rigid or high-performance skis without tacking on excessive weight, the disadvantages of heavy skis are glaring. If two skis offer similar performance, the general rule is that the lighter skis are better (as long as they are made to be durable and don't experience chatter at high speeds). That being said, heavier skis might be something a skier would prefer in specific conditions or circumstances. Weight is just another thing to consider when comparing different styles or models of skis.

Edge shape is the final variable that can influence how your ski will perform. The edges of a ski are made of a metal strip that borders the perimeter of a ski's base. These metal edges are what enables a skier to turn, similar to how the blades of an ice skate enables an ice skater to change direction on a nearly frictionless sheet of ice. One of the biggest innovations in skiing was the introduction of the iconic hourglass shape that skis and snowboards implement today. There was a time where the edges of a ski were completely straight, but those days are long gone. Like flat skis, straight-edged skis are ancient relics that have become obsolete. The hourglass edge shape we use today helps create distinct contact points that easily carve into the snow to enable dynamic turns. Since so many manufacturers have embraced this change, there isn't much more that needs to be said about this topic. That said, there's no harm in learning how edge shape can enhance a skis performance.

Since this sport is constantly evolving, there may be future innovations that become the new industry standard. Longtime skiers know this firsthand. We've seen flat skis, skinny skis, and straight-edged skis rapidly replaced by revolutionary new equipment designs. The next revolutionary innovation in skiing could change how we look at these variables in ski design.

When it comes to modern skis, many of the differences can be subtle. For a beginner or intermediate level skier, these subtle differences will likely go unnoticed. Unless you're an advanced skier looking to optimize performance in specific scenarios or conditions, the typical recommendation is to stick with a standard all-mountain ski that's suited to your height and weight.

Even rental skis, which are notorious for being cheap and clunky compared to high-end models, generally offer outstanding performance that is light-years ahead of the premium ski equipment used in the not-too-distant past. Renting gear is a great option for skiers that are unsure which type of ski they prefer, and renting can help consumers make a more educated decision before purchasing their own pair of skis. Many manufacturers also host events to let riders test their latest equipment firsthand, and some ski resorts also coordinate with these manufacturers to offer equipment demo days. These are just a few ways to experiment with different designs before making a new purchase.

Whichever ski you decide to use, there's a good chance they'll be better than mine! My current skis are over ten years old. That said, it's not the skis that make the skier. These subtle (or sometimes not so subtle) differences shouldn't make too much of a difference in terms of your skiing abilities. Don't spend too much time worrying about which model of ski you'll use. Focus your attention on ensuring your skis are not putting excess strain on your knees or other joints. If that's the case, consider using a smaller or lighter pair of skis as you practice the fundamentals.

BINDINGS

There's not a whole lot to discuss when it comes to ski bindings, as their purpose is simply to lock a skier onto their skis. Whereas differences between various ski models can be subtle, the differences in performance between ski bindings are practically indiscernible. When it comes to ski bindings, the only thing that you should be paying attention to are the types of skiing they're designed for. There are two types of bindings that matter for the purposes of this book: downhill bindings (sometimes called freestyle or alpine bindings) and cross-country ski bindings.

Downhill/freestyle/alpine bindings are the types of bindings most people are familiar with. These are the bindings that lock your feet firmly into your ski once you step into them, and they do not allow your heel to rise. Downhill ski bindings securely attach a skier's feet and are highly effective when skiing down hills.

Cross-country bindings are designed for a different type of skiing. These bindings attach the skier's toes, but allow the heels to rise freely. The detached heel of a cross-country ski binding helps with traversing, climbing, and exploring in snow. Downhill skiing and cross-country skiing are so different, they might as well be considered different sports. Generally speaking, most people who are interested in skiing tend to have downhill skiing in mind.

There are also **hybrid bindings** to consider, which allows a skier to manually attach or detach their heel. Hybrid bindings offer the best of both worlds, giving a skier the option to turn downhill skis into cross-country skis at a moment's notice. The option to detach your heel and turn your downhill skis into cross-country skis seems like a game changer, and although I haven't been able to test these bindings myself I find the concept intriguing. They are definitely on my wish list for new gear to test this upcoming season.

As with any other purchase, read what others are saying before you buy a new pair of bindings to ensure they are right for you. There are plenty of dedicated ski forums online that offer genuine reviews from real customers, which is a great resource for all your ski equipment purchases.

As long as your ski bindings are functional, the differences between various manufacturers or models are practically unnoticeable. The most important decision when choosing a binding is deciding whether you're interested in a cross-country or downhill ski binding. Depending on the type of skiing you plan on doing, you'll likely know which camp you fall into. As you gain more experience you can explore more specialized binding options, such as race bindings, telemark bindings, integrated bindings, or the latest experimental bindings.

We'll talk more about binding settings later on, but for now let's move on and discuss one of the most important pieces of ski equipment.

Ski Boots

Ski boots are one of the most important things to get right when it comes to skiing. There's very little room for error here, as they need to be tight enough to secure your feet but not tight enough to cause issues in circulation. You generally can't just buy a well-reviewed ski boot and hope for the best, you'll need to try them on first and make sure they're as close to perfect for your feet as possible. Even after you've found the perfect fit, ski boots can still be brutally uncomfortable. There is an old joke that snowboarders are just skiers with sensitive feet, and I think that this observation couldn't be more accurate. Snowboard boots tend to be very comfortable, whereas ski boots are notoriously rigid and highly compressive.

There are good reasons for why ski boots have such a reputation. Unfortunately, ski boots need to be tight in order to lock you into your skis. Loose or plushy boots allows for wiggle room, which can quickly lead to an accident or injury (particularly injuries to the knee joints). Your ski boots shouldn't be so tight that they constrict blood flow or cause tingling feet, but they should restrict your foot to the point of being locked tight without any wiggle room. This ensures every motion you make transfers directly into your skis, which is what allows you to control them. They also need to be durable enough to withstand the abuse you'll put them through while skiing, with enough stiffness to provide responsive turning. In other words, the factors that make ski boots uncomfortable are precisely what enhances a skier's performance.

The good news is that the days of uncomfortable ski boots may be over. The old latch-and-clasp system that contributes to uneven tightness may soon go extinct, and I couldn't be happier about that. I was reading an article earlier today about a new design for ski boots that is set to be introduced to the market this year. Instead of using clasps like the ski boots we're currently familiar with, these new boots will implement a BOA system. BOA systems use steel cables that can be manually loosened or tightened, which can help even out pressure points when implemented correctly by the manufacturer. Snowboard boots have used these BOA systems with decent success, but ski boots would require much stronger cables to ensure their durability. We can expect these newer ski boots with BOA systems to solve many of the comfort issues of older ski boot models. While I am eagerly awaiting these new innovations to improve comfort, it's still possible to find latch-and-clasp boots that are comfortable and work well with your feet.

All ski boots essentially function the same way. Their outer linings are made of a hard shell that is designed to attach firmly into your ski bindings. Again, the best way to ensure you find a comfortable pair of ski boots is to have a ski shop measure your feet and test your boots out thoroughly in-store before you buy them. Pay attention to any tight spots or if you have uneven tightness that can't be adjusted. Also be wary of any loose spots, as this will cause painfully irritating friction over time as your feet move around and rub inside the boot while skiing.

Since you'll be wearing ski boots the entire time you are skiing, it is extremely important to choose a boot that will be as comfortable as possible while secured tightly. I cannot stress this enough, so forgive me if I'm starting to sound like a broken record. While ski boots have a reputation for being somewhat uncomfortable when improperly fitted, they are an important piece of equipment that cannot be ignored. While it's normal for your ski boots to be slightly uncomfortable compared to your street shoes, there is an issue if they are painful or if the discomfort is impossible to ignore.

SNOW PANTS, SNOW GLOVES, AND SNOW JACKETS

Any part of your body that could be exposed to the elements should be covered with a waterproof, windproof, and (ideally) insulated shell. These weatherproof outer layers are known as snow pants, snow jackets, and snow gloves. Combined, these individual pieces of equipment cover a skier's body to keep them warm and dry all day long. Your face may need to be protected as well, depending on how bad the weather is. Skiing while wet and cold can be a miserable experience, but in some cases it can also lead to dangerous life-threatening conditions known as hypothermia and frostbite. This is why you'll rarely see people wearing street clothes on the mountain, unless the weather is exceptionally good.

Snow pants are designed to keep snow from reaching your skin or inner clothing layers, as snow will quickly sap a skier's warmth as it melts through to the body's core. Snow pants can resemble your average waist-high pants, but waist-high snow pants have disadvantages in a sport like skiing (mainly snow getting into your butt crack). The most common type of snow pants have suspenders attached, and are sometimes referred to as "snow bibs." The suspenders prevent sagging, stay with you as you move, and the added fabric eliminates the chances of snow getting inside your protective shell (when combined with a snow jacket). Whatever style of snow pants you prefer to wear, make sure that they allow for a full range of motion by doing some squats while wearing them. A slightly loose fit is better than pants that are too tight, as restricted movement in the legs will negatively impact your skiing abilities. It can also be helpful to check that your pants can slip over your ski boots, since that will block snow from reaching your socks or feet.

The **snowboard jacket** goes over your pants to block snow from penetrating into your inner layers, as snow tends to spread into unwanted areas like sand. Like your snow pants and gloves, a good snowboard jacket should be completely waterproof and windproof. Depending on the climate, you may want to consider using a snow jacket that has these qualities plus a high amount of insulation. In my humble opinion, I think it's better to have a snowboard jacket that is too warm rather than too cold. Many snowboard jackets have air vents to manage excess heat, and if you become too warm you can simply unzip the jacket. Any decent ski jacket will be completely waterproof and windproof. Generally speaking, ski jackets with insulation tend to be more expensive. I'm often surprised by how many of my students lack this essential piece of protective equipment when they start taking lessons. Just like with snow pants and snow gloves, ski jackets are an important piece of equipment that shouldn't be ignored.

Snow gloves are one of the most commonly forgotten pieces of equipment, even for people that own them. Since most people tend to not wear gloves in their day-to-day lives, it's easy to forget them when heading to the mountain. It's a good idea to pack an extra pair of gloves in your glovebox (I'm just now realizing why it's called that) or in your riding bag, as you or someone you know are likely to forget a pair of gloves if you keep skiing long enough. Dry gloves are practically a commodity at the ski resort, and having a spare pair is handy if your main pair gets soaked halfway through the day. Regular gloves or work gloves are often not sufficient for skiing, so be sure they are designed for the snow. This means your snow gloves should ideally be waterproof, windproof, and heavily insulated. While having cold hands generally isn't enough to cause hypothermia, cold hands can limit a person's ability to use their fingers. For this reason alone, it should go without saying that gloves are important for a skier's enjoyment, safety, and success.

The combination of snow gloves, snow pants, and a snow jacket creates a protective shell that shields your body from the snow. Since you can bundle multiple layers of clothing underneath your snowsuit as makeshift insulation, the primary goal of this shell is to prevent snow, wind, and snowmelt from reaching your skin. Hypothermia and frostbite are dangerous conditions that could develop if you aren't using adequate snow protection, meaning that your equipment should at the very least be waterproof and windproof. It's also much easier to enjoy this sport when you are comfortable and warm, so this equipment helps maximize a skier's enjoyment on the slopes while staying protected from the elements.

Ski Goggles

Snow is very reflective. The sunlight that is reflected off the snow can damage your eyes indirectly, even when the sun isn't shining brightly. On top of that, snow or ice particles can be flung directly into your eyes from the wind or just from moving around on your skis. Simple sunglasses are generally not enough, as reflected sunlight and tiny ice particles will find their way through the gaps. At best, this can be a frustrating irritation. At worst, your eyes can be damaged or start to look like cooked hamburger meat. This is why ski goggles wrap completely around your face, and why they are highly recommended pieces of equipment. Goggle lenses come in different shades and colors to provide the best visibility in various lighting conditions.

Low-light lenses work best in dark or cloudy lighting, highlighting the otherwise imperceptible differences and subtle shadows in the snow. Snow has a tendency to limit depth perception in low-light conditions, but a good pair of low-light lenses generally resolves this issue. Low-light lenses are commonly yellow, pink, light green, or light blue. Yellow low-light lenses seem to provide the best visibility on hazy days, as they block more blue light from the color spectrum (one of the culprits causing limited depth perception on the snow).

Dark lenses are darker tints than low-light lenses. Darker lenses are better when the sun is shining brightly, as the snow reflects the full intensity of the light. These lenses are usually, for lack of better words, darker or "blacker" than low-light lenses (although there are a few color options for dark lenses). Regardless of which type of lens you're using, any respectable ski goggle brand will provide full UV protection. When looking for a new pair of goggles I recommend choosing snow goggles with the widest field of view, as some goggles can restrict visibility due to their shape. You should also choose a size that works well with your head shape. Additionally, you should ensure that your goggles fit well with your helmet.

One downside of wearing goggles is that they tend to fog up easily. However, there are some things you can do to avoid or resolve this problem. Preventing moisture from getting inside your goggles in the first place is one of the most effective ways to combat fogging issues. Keep your goggles on while skiing to prevent snow or moisture from the air from getting inside. Some jackets or ski masks can vent a skier's breath directly into their goggles, which is something you should anticipate and avoid if possible. There are also various anti-fog products that you can apply to your lenses, and these can be very helpful to prevent moisture buildup. Some goggles even have self-ventilating fans, movement-based ventilation, or heating options to prevent fogging. The goggles I use have lenses that are easily swappable, which I've found to be another effective way to combat fogging issues throughout the day. As you can see, there are various ways to keep your goggles functioning all day long. Since goggles help enhance a skier's vision while offering eye protection, ski goggles are yet another important piece of equipment.

Helmet

A helmet is another essential piece of equipment, yet it's important to understand the limitations of a helmet in a sport like skiing. While they do help protect your head in an accident, the speeds skiers can experience while skiing are great enough that helmets might not fully protect you. This is why it's important to practice on slopes where you can maintain control. A runaway collision with a tree would certainly be a dangerous situation, regardless of your helmet choice.

Ski helmets are functionally the same as bicycle or football helmets, although many ski helmets have added features like adjustable ventilation ducts or clasps to secure ski goggles. Like the helmets used in other sports, some ski helmets are designed to withstand repeated impacts whereas others are only designed to absorb one major impact. A good ski helmet will fit nicely and is shaped to accommodate your ski goggles. Ski helmets also help keep your head warm, so they're safer and more functional than a hat.

MISCELLANEOUS EQUIPMENT

There are several additional pieces of equipment that can be beneficial to include in your ski gear checklist. These miscellaneous odds and ends are optional or inconsequential, depending on your needs as a skier. Regardless, it's a good idea to learn about these miscellaneous pieces of gear if you plan to stick with the sport.

Your **socks and base layers** can be important considerations. Thick or loose socks may easily bunch up inside your ski boots, which can lead to uncomfortable constriction or poor circulation. I recommend wearing thin athletic socks that won't wrinkle as you ski, instead of "winter socks" that will need to be adjusted throughout the day. As for the base layers of clothing you choose to wear underneath your snow jacket or snow pants, there are certain fabrics that are better suited than others in snowy climates. Merino wool, wool, and synthetic blends are some examples of underlayer fabrics that provide reliable warmth and comfort while skiing. These fabrics wick moisture away from your skin and stay relatively warm even if they get wet. Other fabrics can be warm at first, but lose their insulating qualities once sweat or snow accumulates inside your snowsuit. Cotton is a notoriously dangerous fabric for alpine adventurers, and survivalists will tell you that cotton has significant disadvantages in cold or wet climates. That said, cotton clothing can be a great fabric to slip into after you're done skiing.

Face masks are generally optional, but some additional coverage is recommended to protect exposed skin. Balaclavas and ski masks are widely used by skiers for this reason, as they block wind and ice from peppering your face. Scarves can also be a good option, but if you use a scarf make sure that it isn't loose. The last thing you want is a trailing scarf to become snagged on something while you're skiing.

Backpacks or chest packs can be useful for packing extra gear like safety equipment, food, water, compact shovels, whistles, avalanche beacons, or communication devices like short-range radios. As long as your pack isn't too heavy, it shouldn't throw off your balance too much or negatively impact your skiing abilities. A lot of the additional equipment I just listed may be unnecessary for the type of skiing you'll be doing. For example, it's unlikely that you'd need an avalanche beacon as a beginner practicing at a ski resort. If you do bring these additional pieces of safety equipment, it's a good idea to store them in areas you can easily reach. This is especially true for things like whistles or radios, as you might not be able to reach them when you need them most. This is why chest packs are generally considered more useful than backpacks, although each serves a purpose in how you organize extra equipment.

Short-range radio transmitters (more commonly known as walkie-talkies) may seem like outdated technology in the age of cellphones, but these are effective communication tools on the mountain where good cellular service is not guaranteed. They are much more reliable than cellphones in areas with questionable service, which is why you'll see ski patrol using professional-grade radio transmitters instead of alternative communication tools. These communication tools are not only useful for safety reasons, they are also useful for coordinating meetups with friends or family. The utility these devices provide are diverse and I highly recommend them, especially if you are prone to separating from your riding group or have a bad sense of direction (like myself). If you use a walkie-talkie, make sure yours is waterproof and weatherproof.

Hand warmers are another common piece of miscellaneous equipment used by skiers and snowboarders. These can be slipped inside your gloves to keep your hands warm. It's not a requirement, but the additional warmth and comfort they provide can make your skiing experience more enjoyable.

Compact shovels are an optional piece of equipment that has many uses. Shovels can be used in a survival scenario to build shelter or as a rescue tool in an avalanche. They can also be used to build jumps or sculpt features in the snow. Compact shovels can be folded or collapsed to fit easily in or on a backpack, and are practical tools due to their versatility.

There are many pieces of miscellaneous equipment that I haven't mentioned, but discussing them all goes beyond the purpose of this book. If you think of something that would benefit your next ski trip, go ahead and toss it into your ski bag or glovebox. While these additional pieces of equipment are not necessarily required, many of these additions make skiing safer or more enjoyable.

4 Ski Binding Installation and Adjustment

Bindings are the pieces of equipment that attach a skier to their skis via the ski boots. Unfortunately for skiers, the installation of ski bindings is a complicated and somewhat difficult process. The good news is that adjusting your skis is a breeze once the bindings are installed, and you'll rarely have to make adjustments to your bindings as a skier. The only times you would need to adjust your ski bindings is if your boot size changes, if your ski bindings somehow become too loose or too tight, or if you need to change your boot release settings (which are called the DIN settings). If you are using skis with bindings that have already been installed and adjusted, such as the case with rental skis, you can essentially skip this entire chapter and get straight to skiing.

Although it can be a complicated process, setting up your skis is an achievable task for anyone who is handy using tools. The first step, and the most complicated piece of this puzzle, is installing the ski bindings. After that, a simple twist of the screwdriver is all it takes to make adjustments. The heel portion of the binding can be adjusted forward or moved back to securely clasp a ski boot. Adjusting the toe cap of the binding changes the DIN settings, which are the release force settings of the ski bindings.

Before we go through the process of setting up your skis, I should mention that many equipment shops and ski resorts will adjust your equipment or install ski bindings for a small fee (or even for free). New skiers should try to utilize the services of an expert to avoid unnecessary stress and ensure that their ski bindings are properly adjusted or installed. Since these services may not be available where you live, I'm going to spend some time covering this process in detail.

INSTALLING NEW BINDINGS

Installing a new pair of ski bindings is a lengthy and challenging process. It's possible to make a small mistake that could ruin your skis or lead to improperly aligned bindings. While installing your own ski bindings can be a difficult task, it is possible to do it yourself at home. If the skis you're using already have bindings attached, you can skip this section to learn about ski binding adjustments.

Whenever I'm learning something new, I like to use a visual reference as a guide. If you plan to use this book as a reference while installing your ski bindings, I recommend using a tutorial video to aid your efforts. The most useful video I found on the topic is called "How to Mount Your Own Skis" on YouTube, and it was produced by the Ski Sled Shred channel. If you're going to install your own bindings, I highly recommend watching this video or a similar tutorial to help clarify each step. Using these written instructions in addition to a visual guide can help you avoid making potentially expensive mistakes.

Before you start installing your bindings, you'll first need to decide where your bindings will go. Some skis will have a line indicating the recommended binding placement, but not every ski will have this. If there are no guidelines for binding placements on your skis, you essentially have two options. The first option is to mount your bindings in the middle of your skis, which is measured from tip to tail and marked directly on the centerline. This is sometimes called the "true center" of the ski. Alternatively, you can mount your bindings a few centimeters back from the centerline towards the tail-end of your skis, which is referred to as a "traditional mount."

Center mounted skis have certain advantages and disadvantages when compared to skis with traditional mounts. The advantage of center mounted skis is that your center of balance is right where you'd expect it, which makes things like initiating spins and grinding rails feel a little more natural. Center mounted skis would be ideal for acrobatic skiers who are interested in performing tricks, landing switch, spinning, or grinding rails. However, there are disadvantages to center mounted skis. One disadvantage is that the ski tips tend to sink a little easier in deeper snow, as a skier's weight is further forward than it would be on a traditionally mounted ski. Center mounted skis can also be harder to control while turning, which can make executing technical turns more difficult. Because a skier will compensate for this by leaning further back than usual, center mounted skis are less reliable when skiing steep terrain. Since center mounted skis perform best in terrain parks on compact snow, skiers looking for an all-mountain ski setup might prefer a traditionally mounted ski.

Traditionally mounted skis easily float through powder, and the placement of the bindings helps balance the forces a skier experiences while accelerating. While traditionally mounted skis can be slightly resistant to turn initiations, they allow for more aggressive and technical carving (especially at high speeds). Things like spinning or doing tricks may be somewhat more difficult with traditionally mounted skis, however, performing tricks is still possible. For these reasons, I would argue that the strengths of traditionally mounted skis outweigh their weaknesses. Regardless of how you choose to mount your ski bindings, the process for installation is essentially the same.

To install your ski bindings you'll need a tape measure, hammer, pencil, screwdriver, some masking tape, superglue, a speed square, drill bits, and a drill. Start by laying a strip of masking tape down the length of your top sheet (the side of your ski where your bindings and feet touch). Measuring across the width of the ski, use a tape measure to mark the middle of your skis and continue to mark the center every six inches. Draw a lengthwise (vertical) centerline down the length of your ski through the marks you made to help ensure that your bindings will be mounted perfectly centered. You can also measure the ski from tip to tail and mark a horizontal line (widthwise). This horizontal line will be several centimeters back towards the tail for a traditional mount, or directly in the center of your ski for a center mount. Your ski may already have this horizontal line to indicate the recommended binding placement, in which case you can just copy the mark onto the masking tape. Use a speed square tool to ensure the marks you make are lining up perfectly at 90 degrees across the junction of the centerline and the horizontal line. Repeat this process to prep both skis for the next steps.

Now that each ski is taped and marked, lay a fresh strip of masking tape on the bottom of your bindings (both toe caps and heels). Allow the tape to overhang past the edges by a few centimeters so that you can match the new marks we'll make to the masking tape we marked on the ski. Just as we did with the skis, measure the center of your bindings so that you can draw a horizontal and vertical line on each binding. Be sure to extend the line a little beyond the end of the binding into the overhanging masking tape, as extending your marks past the binding will allow us to visually line up the markings to the masking tape on the ski.

Before we go any further, you should take a look at your ski boots. There should be a line or an arrow somewhere along the boot's siding. This arrow or line is where you'll match your ski boot to the horizontal mark indicating the recommended binding placement. The mounting indicator on your boot will help show where the toe cap and heel portions of your bindings will be placed.

Hold the toe cap of your ski binding snugly against the toe of your ski boot, then match your boot's mounting indicator to the horizontal mark on the ski. Mark the position of the toe cap when it matches the marks on your ski's masking tape. With this additional mark, you can remove the ski boot from the equation. Once you have the position marked and your centerlines match, apply glue to the binding's masking tape (the non-sticky side) and press the binding in place. Wait until the glue dries, as you don't want the alignment to shift while we're completing the next steps.

Now that your toe cap is centered and temporarily glued in place, you'll need to mark the holes where we'll be drilling. It's not a good idea to screw directly into the skis without pre-drilling the holes, so this step will help us attach the bindings without damaging the skis. While you could technically drill directly through the tape into the ski, it's not recommended and drilling through the tape could cause issues. Instead, you should mark the drilling points through the tape with a hammer and a drill bit. Use a drill bit that fits perfectly through the mounting holes without any wiggle room, as you want these marks to be precise. When you've found a drill bit that fits perfectly, strike the drill bit into your ski through the toe cap's mounting holes with your hammer. Rotate the drill bit slightly after each strike, which will make a precise pattern like a crosshair. The makeshift crosshair marks the exact point you'll drill into your ski's top sheet. By rotating the drill bit after every strike, you'll decrease the chances of drilling in the wrong spot. This is why you want to use a drill bit that fits perfectly inside the binding, as your marks could otherwise become misaligned. Once all four of the mounting holes in your toe cap are marked, you can peel off the masking tape under the toe cap and move onto the next step.

To precisely drill the proper depth of the mounting screw holes, you'll need to place the mounting screws into the toe cap and measure the length of the screw that pokes past the bottom of the binding. Match the length to your drill bit and mark to the ideal depth. You can line up a small piece of masking tape to the depth mark on your drill bit to visually indicate the point where you should stop drilling. With that piece of tape as a visual marker, you'll easily be able to observe if you start drilling too deep. You'll also want to make sure that your drill bit is not too wide for the screws the bindings use, as the mounting screws will need something to grab into. Calipers can be a handy tool for this step, as they can ensure precise depth and width measurements. With these preparations, you can precisely drill the mounting screw holes directly into the top sheet of the ski.

Clean up the rough edges of the drilled holes with a razor or knife, and then place a small dab of glue in the drilled holes. This seals the areas you drilled into and will help the bindings sit perfectly flush. Put the toe caps back into place and screw the bindings down by hand before the glue has time to dry. You could use a drill for this step, however, installing the toe caps by hand helps prevent stripping issues or unnecessary damage to the ski. After all four binding screws are firmly attached, your toe cap is installed.

Your rear bindings can be tightened or loosened, which can be helpful if your boot size changes. Before you install your rear bindings, adjust them so that there is room to loosen or tighten the bindings once they're installed. You'll want to do this before we actually attach the rear bindings, because the adjustment positions will be locked-in once they are installed. This means that you won't be able to loosen or tighten your bindings if they are already adjusted to the loosest or tightest position. Make sure both your bindings are adjusted to matching positions, and provide some extra room to loosen the bindings if your feet are still growing. Once you're finished, draw a centerline on the bottom of your rear bindings using the same masking tape method we utilized for the toe caps.

Place your ski boot into the toe cap you just installed, and slide the rear binding forward until the heel of your boot fits the step-in portion of your rear binding. Mark the position, then match the centerlines of the masking tape that's placed on your ski and rear binding. Glue the position down once the lines match, just like you did for the toe cap. Mark the holes using a drill bit and a hammer, and repeat the same process we previously discussed to drill the holes for your rear binding's mounting screws. Clean up the holes with your razor, add a dab of glue, and manually screw your bindings down using a screwdriver.

Test your work by stepping into your binding with a ski boot, just as you normally would on a ski slope. Tighten the bindings if there is any wiggle room. If the bindings are too tight, loosen the bindings until you can successfully clip your boots in. If something seems off but your bindings are properly installed, check the DIN settings on the toe cap to make sure that the release force settings aren't too loose or too tight. Detailed instructions on these adjustments are covered in the next sections. After you've finished this final step, repeat the process to install the bindings onto your second ski.

As you can see, this is not the easiest job for most people to accomplish. A lot of things can potentially go wrong, which is why having a gear expert handle this process for you is recommended. If you do install your own bindings, I highly recommend following the tutorial video I mentioned at the start of this section. The Ski Sled Shred channel on YouTube goes into greater detail, provides a visual reference, and does an excellent job of walking you through the process.

Luckily, adjusting your DIN settings and adjusting your bindings is easy once the bindings are installed. We can breeze through the next sections of this chapter with ease.

ADJUSTING YOUR BINDINGS

To adjust your ski bindings, all you need is a screwdriver. Most ski bindings are adjusted with a single screw in the heel section that slides the binding forward or backward. Other ski bindings may use two screws instead of one, but the process is essentially the same. Simply turn your screwdriver clockwise to tighten your bindings, or counterclockwise to loosen them. Check your work by clipping your ski boots into your bindings. Ensure that everything is properly secured by jostling your skis around.

You'll know when you need to adjust your bindings when you either cannot step into your binding to attach them, or if your boot wiggles at all once it's clipped in. If you cannot step into your bindings they are most likely too tight. If you notice any gaps or movement between your boot and ski bindings while attached, then your binding is too loose.

ADJUSTING YOUR DIN SETTINGS

DIN settings are the industry-adopted scale for the release force settings of ski bindings. DIN is an acronym that stands for "Deutsches Institut für Normung" (German Institute for Standardization). In other words, the DIN settings determine how easily your skis detach. If the DIN settings are too high then the skis will not detach, potentially increasing the likelihood of an injury. If the DIN settings are too low then the skis will detach too easily, increasing the likelihood of a crash. You can see what your current DIN settings are by looking at the dial or meter on your toe cap. The DIN settings can be adjusted easily with the turn of a screwdriver.

Adjustable DIN settings are an important safety feature. You can probably imagine how destructive skiing could potentially become if your skis were locked too tightly, transferring shearing forces or impacts directly into your joints. Yet if the DIN settings are set too low, skiing becomes impossible because the slightest movement leads to a detached ski.

Your recommended DIN setting will depend on your weight, ability level, and height. Your age may also lead you to choose a different DIN setting, depending on the type of skiing you're doing and how prone to injury you are. Small children are at the lowest end of the scale, because they can rarely generate the type of force needed to detach from their skis. Beginners below 100 lbs (45 kgs) should generally set their DIN settings somewhere between 1 and 5. Heavier people (up to 165 lbs or 75 kgs) usually need higher DIN settings, and the general recommendation is somewhere between 2 and 7. The highest DIN settings are only recommended in niche circumstances, or for exceptionally tall or heavy people. There are several DIN setting calculators available online, which will give you a fairly accurate recommendation based on the expected forces your body will generate while skiing.

Expert skiers will most likely prefer a higher DIN setting, so that their skis never come off unless they remove their skis themselves. The last thing you want is for your skis to detach while descending a steep slope. Since beginner-level skiers are prone to crashing, lower DIN settings are considered safer while practicing on relatively small slopes.

Similar to adjusting your rear bindings, the DIN settings are easily adjusted. There should be an exposed screw on the front of your toe cap, and you simply need to loosen or tighten this screw with a screwdriver to adjust the DIN settings. The dial or meter on your toe cap that displays your current DIN settings will change as you tighten or loosen the toe cap screw.

The point of adjustable DIN settings is to prevent injury, and the correct DIN setting will depend on things like your weight, height, age, and the type of skiing you are doing. Fortunately, DIN settings can be adjusted quickly without taking too much time away from the slopes. Most ski resorts leave a few screwdrivers in key locations so that you can make adjustments if needed.

5 ARE SKI POLES NECESSARY?

What's the deal with those poles skiers carry? Before we discuss how to ski, let's quickly talk about ski poles. While they are useful for a variety of reasons, ski poles are not required to learn how to ski. For this reason, I won't be talking about them in much detail when discussing lesson progression. Whether or not you choose to use them, there are a few things that skiers should know about ski poles.

The act of skiing is a dynamic form of motion that primarily relies on your leg muscles and abdominal muscles. Since skiing doesn't rely on the muscles in your arms, you can ski perfectly fine without using poles. However, poles can be helpful when used correctly. Most notably, you'll find that poles can be helpful when skiing through flat sections, as a skier can use their poles to push themselves forward. This is especially useful for moving through the lines of a chairlift. Poles can also be used to initiate turns, as putting your pole forward and allowing the tip to contact the snow can help rectify poor skiing posture. The poles themselves aren't contributing to the turning motion, but this act of "pole planting" helps remind some skiers how turns are supposed to work on the snow. Why? Pole planting subconsciously helps skiers embrace a proper skiing stance, which is best described as a subtle downhill-leaning athletic stance. Pole planting "tricks" the body into embracing a slightly forward-leaning position, which is sometimes beneficial for people learning how to ski.

If poles can be helpful, why would some skiers choose not to use them? The primary reason a skier might not use poles is that they can get in the way, especially for skiers who are focused on doing tricks or landing jumps. People with shoulder injuries may also find that they aren't able to utilize their poles properly, which is another good reason why someone would choose not to use them. For some skiers, ski poles are more of a burden than a benefit.

Certain ski instructors may even recommend not using poles, mainly because some students try to use their poles to slow down. Using your poles to slow down is a very bad idea, as this can cause shoulder injuries by putting excessive strain on the shoulder joints. Using your poles to slow down is also extremely ineffective, which is another reason why a ski instructor would teach the fundamentals of turning and braking before allowing their students to use poles.

To measure your recommended pole length, stand straight and let your arms hang down. Your recommended pole length will be roughly around the height of your elbow. When skiing with poles, keep your pole handles slightly forward from your hips. Always keep the tips of your poles pointed backwards (towards your tail-end) as you ski. To use your poles when turning, flick the tip forward and gently let it touch the snow in front of you. If you have a good grasp on how to turn (more on this later), then you should be able to carve your edges around the pole. As you ski past your pole, it will move behind you until the pole tip releases. This effectively returns the poles to the starting point, which prepares a skier for the next turn.

Whether or not you choose to use poles is ultimately up to you. Personally I find them useful, although I mostly use them while waiting in line for chairlifts. While they can be used to help correct bad skiing form, they are not always beneficial for skiers learning how to turn. If you do choose to use them, be careful not to rely on them as brakes. Using your poles to slow down can easily injure your shoulder joints, even at low speeds. If you find that ski poles are getting in the way of your skiing, or if you have a previous shoulder injury that limits the use of poles, you might want to avoid using them.

6 How to Ski (Downhill/Freestyle Skiing)

It's the moment you've all been waiting for. This chapter will detail the fundamental techniques, athletic concepts, and recommended lesson progression taught by reputable ski schools. These are things that a skier would expect to cover in a typical lesson with a ski instructor.

Before detailing the stages of lesson progression, let's briefly summarize the goals of this chapter. The first goal is to provide a safe, effective path to familiarize students with the snow. The second goal is to describe the motions that skiers use to become successful, efficient skiers. The final goal is to apply the knowledge until it makes sense in practice.

Understanding the goals can give readers a significant advantage over others, potentially helping students avoid the common mistakes that most beginners tend to make. Research has shown that visualizing athletic movements can help develop expertise in a variety of sports. This chapter is intended to assist future practice sessions by teaching and describing the proper motions behind skiing.

To elaborate on this idea, let's take a step back and start from square one. What would happen if you took a ski and let it glide downhill by itself? The answer is that the ski would point itself downhill, simply accelerating onward while following the path of least resistance. Skiers embrace that natural movement while adding directional guidance to control the descent. In other words, a ski without a skier essentially becomes a boat without a captain.

In order to change direction and ski properly, a skier uses the metal edges of the skis like rudders on a boat. Remember, the edges of a ski refers to the metal strip lining the bottom perimeter of each ski. Because the base of a ski is practically frictionless, the metal edges of a ski must be utilized to guide movement. This concept is important to understand how the act of skiing actually works. Just like with ice skating, the sharpened metal is what allows a person to turn or stop. Unlike ice skaters, however, skiers have twice as many edges underfoot.

Let's get a little more specific now. The forward edges of the skis must be emphasized to effectively guide your direction. Most beginning skiers (and snowboarders) tend to lean backwards and resist the inevitable downhill acceleration. This is a natural inclination, because it's our instinct to counteract a sudden change of forward movement by leaning back. However, this natural reaction works against a skier, as the exact opposite motion is needed in order to properly turn. The forward edges of a ski are more easily utilized from a centered or a slightly forward athletic stance. Since the forward edges of the skis guide our turns, you can start to see the problem. You can think of this counterintuitive instinct to lean back like a bicycle doing a wheelie, where it's easier to guide the bike when both wheels are touching the ground. In order to get both wheels back on the ground, a skier needs to lean forward instead of leaning back. The front wheel of our bike, or in this case our ski's forward edges, is what allows the rider to turn more reliably.

While we will revisit these ideas throughout our lessons, an understanding of these concepts can help students visualize a more effective way to control their skis. Keeping these concepts in mind, the strategy for turning first-time skiers into experts can be broken down into five stages of progression. Take your time with these lessons, and only progress to the next stage once you feel comfortable with the skills being discussed. Remember that progressing your skills as a skier will take time and practice, so have fun with the process and enjoy the journey!

THE FIVE STAGES OF

PROGRESSION

STAGE 1: FLAT LAND DRILLS

Skiing, like most movement-based sports, is a sport that can be hard to practice at low speeds. Everyone knows that it's easier to balance on a bicycle at riding speeds, and skiing is no different. Unfortunately, the sensation of sliding on skis is so unnatural that it would be irresponsible and dangerous to send students straight to the hills. Instead, lessons with first-time skiers should start on a flat patch of snow.

By strapping on a pair of skis and moving around in flat snow, skiers can accommodate to this novel sensation before attempting to conquer steeper terrain. Especially for people who have little experience moving on frictionless surfaces like snow or ice, it's a good idea to familiarize oneself with the feeling of sliding on a relatively manageable scale. In my experience, this initial introduction to skiing is the fastest path to teaching first-timers how to ski like a pro.

To start this lesson, attach your skis and check that there are no issues with the equipment. Some issues that would be concerning are loose boots or bindings, which could increase the chance of a ligament injury and would make controlling the skis more difficult. If there are no issues with your gear, it's time to take the first steps (pun intended) and become comfortable walking on skis in the snow.

Walking on skis can be done in two ways, both of which utilize the metal edges lining the skis. The first way is called "sidestepping," which uses the left or right edges of each ski in tandem to walk laterally instead of forwards. On flat land you should get used to this pretty quickly, as you'll barely have to engage your edges to provide adequate traction. When you practice sidestepping on skis, start by tilting both skis to the right to grip the snow and sidestep laterally to the right. To sidestep left, tilt your skis to the left to engage your ski's left edges. If you are looking to challenge yourself, try sidestepping up a small but gradual slope. You'll discover that you can indeed walk uphill on snow by sidestepping, as long as you keep your skis horizontal to the fall line and utilize your edges by leaning or tilting yourself uphill. We'll do more of this practice later on steeper hills. You should practice this skill until you're comfortable walking sideways on flat land.

The other way a skier can walk on snow is called "duck walking." To duck walk on skis, angle your skis outward by bringing your heels in and pointing your toes out (away from your body). When done correctly, you'll be providing yourself traction by gripping the snow with the inner edges of your skis (the edges that run along the side of your big toe on each foot). Like sidestepping, you can use this method to walk up small hills and across icy terrain. Duck walking has limitations in steeper terrain, however, duck walking can be used to gain speed by pushing off one foot and gliding with the other. Practice duck walking until you're comfortable walking on flat snow. After becoming accustomed to duck walking and sidestepping, we can start to familiarize ourselves to the unusual sensation of skiing by practicing gliding.

Gliding on flat snow requires a skier to use their inside ski's edges to gain speed, which are the same edges used to duck walk in the previous drill. To glide, push the inside edge of one ski to slide on the other ski. Using each ski in combination provides traction and forward motion. Alternate pushing off each foot and gliding with the other, with the goal of maintaining your speed. If you're familiar with ice skating or hockey, you understand that this motion is practically identical to what we're aiming for as skiers practicing gliding. Gliding on flat snow will help you understand the delicate balance between using your edges and balancing on the flat base of your skis. If you're struggling to glide using a duck walk to the point of frustration, I recommend practicing gliding on a small slope instead of a flat patch of snow. This will enable you to practice gliding at similarly low speeds without having to gain momentum by pushing or duck walking. Learning how to glide using a duck walk is not an essential part of skiing, it just provides an opportunity to practice turning in a safe space without picking up excessive speeds.

Turning is a difficult skill to learn, and we'll be practicing our turns at every stage of progression. For our introduction to turning, our practice will require us to pick up some speed. You can use the duck walk method of gliding to practice turning, or as I mentioned previously you can practice turning on a very small hill. The only reason I recommend starting on flat snow is to avoid gaining potentially overwhelming speeds. Regardless of how you prefer to practice, turning can be learned in two ways.

The first way is actually an improper turning technique, but it does provide beginners a number of benefits. Since the improper turning technique can be used as an emergency brake and teaches students how to utilize their edges, many instructors still choose to teach this skill. This technique is called the "pizza wedge," as the skiing stance resembles a pizza wedge shape when utilized. To practice the pizza wedge, point your toes together and emphasize the inside edges of your skis to scrape into the snow (the edges lining your big toe on each foot). If equal amounts of pressure are applied to each edge, the skis will act as a brake to slow you down. However, you can choose to put more weight on one edge to initiate a pizza wedge turn. The turning motion is due to the guiding forces of the weighted edge, which will rotate a skier as the ski carves a path in the snow. While there are some benefits of learning the edge control utilized in the pizza wedge technique, relying on this technique is ineffective for turning and braking at more advanced levels.

The proper turning technique is more difficult to learn, especially at low speeds. We're going to practice the proper technique regardless of this fact, as there are a number of issues with the pizza wedge technique. A proper turn requires your skis to be parallel to each other and pointing straight ahead. To practice a proper turn, glide forward and tilt both skis left (to turn left) or right (to turn right). This tilting motion shouldn't be confused with leaning sideways.

Instead of leaning sideways to turn, lean slightly forward and put pressure on your shins while subtly guiding the tilting motion left or right. This forward pressure into your ski boots transfers your body's energy forward and allows your forward edges to guide a turn with very little tilting motion of the skis. If you're having difficulty practicing proper turns, try bouncing forward repeatedly onto the tips of your toes throughout the turn. This motion can help engage the edges while keeping the skis parallel. Proper turns are more difficult to practice at low speeds, but if you can master this type of turn now it will be easier to apply proper turns in more difficult terrain. In steeper terrain the pizza wedge method can be dangerous, which is why it's important to practice proper turns early in our development. Again, don't worry if you're struggling at this stage of our practice. We'll practice this skill later on. For now, we're just beginning to build skiing motions into our muscle memory.

Braking is another difficult skill to apply properly, because efficient braking requires a skier to skillfully apply the proper turning technique. Thankfully, the improper "pizza wedge" turning technique can be used to slow down, turn, and stop. It's okay to use the pizza wedge in the early stages of development. In later lessons, we'll practice proper braking techniques until they're more natural.

Using the brakes isn't quite as simple on skis compared to using something like bicycle brakes, as skis technically don't have brakes. That being said, there are three ways skiers can effectively stop a descent. The first way a skier can slow down is by turning. Turns can be combined to consistently and gradually reduce gained speed. Turns can also be held to angle the skis uphill, which is a reliable way to transition from a turn into a full stop. The next way a skier can brake is an advanced technique called the "hockey stop," something that we will practice in later lessons. Hockey stops are sometimes referred to as "power slides," and it's essentially the same motion that hockey players or ice skaters use to stop quickly. Hockey stops are generally the fastest way to stop, but it's something a skier will have to practice once they have more control of their edges. The final way to slow down and stop on skis is the iconic pizza wedge technique! While the pizza wedge is the least efficient way to slow down or stop, it can be a valuable technique in the event a skier loses control. While the pizza wedge is a controversial skill that can lead to bad ski habits, it is a reliable braking method at low speeds and on small hills. Just remember that a reliance on the pizza wedge technique is problematic and can lead to accidents, as the effectiveness of this method is greatly reduced in steeper terrain. Many instructors believe that the pizza wedge teaches important concepts early on, while also providing a safety net for students who feel they are losing control on small slopes.

Turning and braking is not a skill most people will learn overnight, so practice these techniques on flat snow or small hills until you feel somewhat comfortable initiating turns and slowing down. The goal of these lessons is to get a skier accustomed to the snow before moving onto the next steps, and we will practice these fundamental skills in the next lessons to eventually become experts at proper turning and braking techniques.

Let's do a quick summary of what we've learned so far. The first thing we practiced is simply walking on the snow, which requires using your ski's edges to step laterally (sidestepping) or to walk forward (duck walking). We then practiced gliding like an ice skater, pushing off our edges to propel forward with a little bit of speed. Using our forward momentum, we then performed two types of turns at low speeds. For "proper turns," the skis are straight and a forward-leaning or bouncing motion initiates our turns. Subtly titling the left-side ski edges turns our skis to turn left, while tilting the right-side ski edges turns us to the right. Turning by using the pizza wedge is the "improper turn." A pizza wedge turn uses the weight placed on a skier's inner edges (the edges lining the big toes) to guide turns. Using the pizza wedge technique, putting more weight on the inner-left ski edge turns the skier to the right. More weight on the inner-right ski edge turns a skier to the left. Finally, we talked about how braking works as a beginner. At this stage of learning, turning is the best way to slow down and stop. However, the pizza wedge technique can help a skier grind to a halt while they are learning how to turn. Because the pizza wedge is highly ineffective and potentially dangerous when used on steep slopes, you should try to avoid relying on this technique.

With these initial lessons you should be gaining more awareness of how a skier uses their edges to turn. If you take a look at each ski individually, you might start to see how we've been using our edges to turn. As you can see, the left edge of a ski turns the ski to the left, while the right edge is used to turn right. The same is true when pairing your skis together.

While these flat land drills may seem unnecessary, this warm-up does three things. The first thing it does is help reduce the fear response that sliding on skis can trigger by giving some sense of control back. It also helps students become more familiar with the edges of their skis, and how they are utilized to affect movement. The final thing this warmup does is provide the foundational skills that could help a skier stay safe if they ever encounter a slope that is too difficult for their skill level. For example, sidestepping is a skill that could be used to climb away from dangerous terrain. While it may seem silly to practice skiing on flat snow, don't underestimate the importance of these early lessons. It might not be glamorous, but these flat land drills help provide a framework to learn while avoiding scary situations or potential hazards in the environment. We'll be revisiting these fundamental concepts in later lessons as we continue to practice and improve over time.

Since there's only so much you can learn on a flat patch of snow, it won't be long before you're ready to advance onto the next stage of progression. When you feel somewhat confident maneuvering on flat snow, feel free to move onto the next lessons. Don't worry if you haven't mastered all of these concepts, as the goal of flat land drills is simply to introduce skiers to the sport. Once you have a rudimentary understanding of how to control your skis on flat snow, you should be qualified to start taking the next steps in a safe and controlled manner.

STAGE 2: SAFETY SLIPS, TRAVERSALS, TURNING, AND STOPPING

The next stage of progression teaches new fundamental skills and safety techniques that skiers will find useful throughout their development. Instead of practicing on a flat patch of snow, these drills should be practiced on small hills. The ideal practice hill will be a gradual, manageable slope that ends with a flat section. A practice hill with these qualities will prevent students from losing complete control while practicing. The new skills we'll be learning next are sideslips and traversals. We'll also practice braking and turning to help improve control over the skis.

Sideslipping, which is also called the "falling leaf method," is when you slide sideways downhill while keeping your skis horizontal to the slope (as opposed to pointing the skis downhill). This can be handy for getting out of tricky spots, as it allows you to descend in a fairly controlled manner without much acceleration. There are some limitations to this technique, but it's worth practicing because it helps a skier understand how to use their edges to reliably control their direction. Learning how sideslipping works is also a stepping stone to teach more advanced braking techniques, such as power slides (also known as hockey stops).

To practice sideslipping, start by sidestepping up a small hill. To ascend a hill by sidestepping, a skier will need to tilt their skis slightly uphill so that the uphill edges can provide traction. Transitioning from a sidestep to a sideslip is easy, simply tilt the skis slightly downhill to the point where the ski's edges lose their hold. This will allow a skier to slip down the hill while remaining lateral to the fall line of a slope. To stop slipping sideways, tilt your skis back to the original uphill-leaning position that was used to sidestep. This motion reapplies the edges and allows a skier to regain their traction. Combining sidestepping with sideslipping is a great way to build muscle memory and teaches a skier how their edges can be used to control the skis.

For a more detailed explanation of sideslipping, let's use the example of a person sidestepping to the left to climb up a small hill. In this situation, the skis would also be tilted to the left to provide traction (using the edges on the left side of the skis). In this situation, the skier would simply tilt their skis to the right to start slipping sideways. To stop sideslipping in this example, the skier would then tilt their skis to the left to re-engage the left sides of their edges and halt their descent. Although this sounds complicated, combining sidestepping with sideslipping will simplify this lesson and reduce the chance of making a mistake. The reason for combining these skills in our practice is that sidestepping requires a skier to utilize proper edge control, while sideslipping is only possible when the skier disengages those edges. Be sure to practice sideslipping in both directions, which will help build beneficial muscle memory on both sides of your body.

There are some limitations when applying this skill. Sideslipping in icy conditions can be unreliable, as the ski's edges will not grip into solid ice or provide traction as easily. Sideslipping on icy surfaces could lead to a crash, a potentially hazardous slide, or cause a skier to lose their balance. Sideslipping is also an unreliable technique in extremely steep terrain. That being said, sideslipping is an important concept to learn as a skier. Sideslipping is a useful safety technique that can be utilized frequently and will benefit any skier's development.

Traversing is the act of skiing laterally across the ski slope, instead of following the downhill fall line. Traversing across a ski slope can be beneficial for avoiding hazards and finding more favorable paths downhill. A skier can also use traversals to gain speed or slow down quickly. For this lesson, we'll practice a controlled traversal by angling our skis horizontally across the hill.

Before we begin, we should remember the rider guidelines. Although other skiers should be providing ample room for you to traverse, it is not always easy for other people to predict a traversing rider's movements. Always look uphill before starting a traversal, and never traverse underneath a jump or into locations where others cannot see you. If possible, practice your traversals in an area where there are fewer riders to avoid a potential collision.

When practicing traversals, keep your skis horizontal across the fall line. To pick up speed, simply angle your skis slightly downhill. You'll find that traversing across the hill is something that can be achieved fairly easily, as the angle of your skis will barely change before the skis pick up speed and begin to travel laterally. Once you have sufficient speed, angle your skis slightly uphill to come to a gradual stop. If you're having trouble angling your skis while practicing traversals, it might be a sign that you need more practice turning. Some skiers will lean backward to change the angle of their skis, but proper turning requires you to embrace a centered or slightly forward-leaning stance. Controlling the skis through an athletic stance is a more effective way of guiding the skis, so keep this in mind while practicing traversals. For students who are struggling, I'll ask them to bounce on their toes through the traversal. This is a simple tip that helps students shift their weight into a riding stance, which gives them more control while skiing.

It's also important to remember that each ski has a left and right edge. You'll be favoring your left edges to maintain a traversal to the left, while using your right edges to maintain a traversal to the right. Practice traversing in both directions to develop muscle memory, ensuring that traversals can be executed whenever they are needed. Being able to traverse in both directions provides a skier more freedom to navigate the mountain or avoid dangerous terrain.

Because traversing requires a skier to resist the path of least resistance, traversals can be exhausting to practice. It is normal to become tired quickly when practicing this skill. Maintaining a traversal for a long time can demand a large effort from the leg muscles, so don't be alarmed if your muscles begin to cramp. Take breaks and return to this lesson after your body has time to recover. The goal of this drill is to learn how traversals can be used to speed up, slow down, and come to a stop. Once you're comfortable controlling your skis while traversing in both directions, we can move onto the next lesson.

Turning and stopping are skills that are closely related to each other. These skills are learned gradually, and applying correct turning and braking techniques is easier said than done. For this lesson, we'll focus on practicing the more effective form of stopping and turning. While it's true that the pizza wedge technique can provide a helpful foundation for beginners, it's important that we practice the correct technique. When it comes to turning and braking, the proper technique is more effective, safer, and more reliable than the pizza wedge technique. Turning and stopping correctly are two of the most important foundational skills for skiers.

To begin our lesson, find a practice hill that provides enough room to gather speed in a safe and controlled way. Ideally, this hill will end with a flat section as a safety precaution. Start by pointing both skis downhill, then pick a direction to turn while keeping the skis parallel to each other (instead of a pizza wedge shape). In order to drive our leading edges and guide our turns properly, adopt a slightly forward-leaning athletic stance with your weight placed over the toes. Remember, this stance is what allows skiers to control their skis and utilize their edges effectively. If you've ever watched a downhill ski race, you can see that the proper skiing stance embraces this forward-leaning stance. That being said, at our current stage of development you don't need to emphasize this forward-leaning stance as much as downhill ski racers do. Once you've adopted an athletic skiing stance, the way to initiate a turn is to shift your body to favor weight on one ski over the other. It's worth mentioning that you still need to be balanced on both skis, but the slight difference in force applied to the skis should often be enough to initiate a turn. This idea is similar to how turning works with the pizza wedge, except we'll be using an outside edge to turn in addition to one of the inside edges. You can also try tilting your skis if that helps you engage your edges, just be careful not to overdo it and stop if you experience any pain in your joints.

Let's take a moment to visualize the difference between "improper" and "proper" turns. In earlier lessons, we discovered how applying more weight to one ski could guide a turn while using the pizza wedge technique. The reason this happens is that the inside edge of the weighted ski is pushed into the snow, which is the guiding edge that carves the turn. Compare this to what happens when the skis are kept straight. In this scenario, there are two guiding edges instead of just one. Putting more weight on the left edges turns the skis to the left, whereas weight on the right edges turns the skis to the right. Improper turns are unreliable and ineffective in more advanced terrain, whereas proper turns are reliable at high speeds and steep terrain. A proper turn is only achieved when a skier embraces the downhill motion of skiing, as this is what it takes to apply the leading edges that are located towards the nose-end of the skis.

Both types of turns rely on the ski's edges to change direction or slow down, however, advancing to the next stages of progression will require a skier to apply the correct edges to turn on command. Learning this skill will require a significant amount of practice hours, although some students embrace this concept quickly. The students who learn this skill quickly are typically exhilarated by the sensation of speed. They embrace the feeling of sliding and are eager to take control of their forward movement by leaning into the downhill momentum, whereas most people (myself included) resist that unnatural sensation of sliding as beginners.

Again, this is a difficult concept to learn, which is why I'm taking the time to repeat myself throughout these instructions. It will take a lot of practice and repetition until the concepts and motions I'm describing make sense. It will also take a lot of practice for a person to develop the muscle memory necessary to make this type of skiing feel more natural. It is challenging to internalize the nuanced motions that a skier uses. The ideas should start to make more sense with enough time on the snow. After becoming more comfortable with proper turns, you can stop relying on the pizza wedge technique as much. Once you've achieved this goal, we can progress to the next step and apply this skill to improve our stopping abilities.

In order to practice **stopping** more quickly and efficiently, we'll be using our newfound turning skills. Start on a hill from a full stop, where your skis are horizontal to the downhill slope. From this starting position, point the skis downhill and initiate a turn. Maintain the turn to carve a big C-shape in the snow. A complete C-shape will point the skis laterally across the hill (opposite of the direction your skis started in). To slow down enough to stop, you'll have to angle your skis slightly uphill. In essence, this is the same way we practiced stopping during our traversals, where skiing or traversing uphill can be used to slow down and eventually stop. The difference here is that we're stopping at the end of a turn, which is how an expert skier often stops themselves when descending a hill. Practice stopping at the end of a C-turn in both directions. Skiers will likely favor turning on one side over the other, and we need to overcome that preference so that it doesn't become an issue later on.

C-turns are an effective way to maintain control when applied correctly, as turning is one of the best ways a skier can reliably slow down or stop. While students at this stage should be encouraged to practice this skill without relying on the pizza wedge, this is easier said than done. It may take some time before a student is comfortable enough to stop using the pizza wedge technique. Like all learned skills, plenty of practice is needed in order to perfect the proper turning and stopping technique.

Once a student can reliably turn and stop in both directions using proper form, they will have reached a significant milestone in their development. It would be acceptable to start teaching the next stage of progression, which involves linking C-turns into S-turns. However, there is an additional method of braking we can begin to practice for those who are interested. This advanced braking technique combines two techniques we learned in previous lessons. C-turning and sideslipping skills can be combined to teach the infamous "power slide" or "hockey stop." As I had mentioned, the power slide is an advanced stopping technique that can be used to stop quickly. Hockey players or ice skaters should be familiar with this skill, as the movements are practically identical.

To practice **power slides**, utilize the edgework we practiced in the sideslipping lesson at the end of a turn. In other words, once a skier is finishing their C-turn they can emphasize their uphill edges into the snow to power slide. For reference, the skier will emphasize their right edges at the end of their right C-turns, and the left edges at the end of their left C-turns. Just like when we were practicing sideslipping, forcing weight onto these edges will cause the skis to come to a sudden halt. This emphasized edgework could be described as a "sitting" motion that puts weight on your uphill-leaning edges, and by sitting (or squatting) your weight onto the uphill edge you provide a sudden increase of traction that halts your forward progress. Power slides are an advanced method of stopping that we'll practice more in future lessons, so don't worry if you can't get the hang of it just yet. Applying a hockey stop is not necessary to move onto the next stage of progression, it is optional practice for students who are interested in learning how power sliding works.

In the next lesson, we'll start practicing on longer runs in order to start linking fundamental skiing skills together. As always, use your best discretion to determine if more advanced terrain is within your ability level.

STAGE 3: LINKING MULTIPLE TURNS

Now that you've learned how to initiate and hold proper turning technique to slow down and stop, we're going to start applying these skills on longer runs. Our primary goal at this stage is to link multiple turns together without coming to a complete stop. That being said, don't hesitate to stop or slow down if you feel like you're gaining too much speed or losing control. It takes many hours of practice to fully absorb these lessons while progressing, so be safe while building towards this eventual goal.

In the previous lesson, we were making large C-shaped turns in the snow. The next step is to practice linking those C-shapes together to achieve S-shaped turns. Alternating turns in this way is how skiers maintain control and reduce excessive speeds as they ski down the mountain over extended distances. While this sounds like an easy and straightforward step, it is not the easiest lesson for most skiers. The ability to chain turns is a difficult step, however, the exciting news is that people who can achieve this task will be one step closer to becoming an expert skier.

S-shaped turns are not necessarily more difficult to initiate, as the fundamental skills of turning are the same motions we will be applying. The challenge is that these turns require higher speeds to maintain, which triggers a person's instincts to resist downhill motion and kicks that feeling into overdrive. Where we could practice C-turns at relatively low speeds, linking multiple C-turns into S-turns means that our skis will be angled downhill for the majority of the time we're skiing. The added acceleration can be jarring for some people. This is why it's important to practice S-turns on a hill that is comfortably sloped and within your ability level. Ideally, the slope will be similar to what we were previously practicing on, although the length of the hill should be longer to provide more room for linking multiple turns. As long as you are comfortable with the ski run, you should have the skills needed to succeed.

In order to turn C-turns into S-turns, skiers need to embrace that infamous forward-leaning stance to effectively guide your edges and lead turns. I know that I sound like a broken record at this point, but it's important to repeat this idea until the motions become natural. Embracing the forward motion of skiing, instead of resisting the feeling of sliding, is the best way to take control of your skis and make them do your bidding.

There are two common mistakes skiers at this stage of progression will make. The first mistake skiers will make is leaning back too much, and since we've talked about this multiple times we probably don't need to elaborate on this idea much further. Obviously leaning back will prevent your leading edges from properly engaging. Leaning back on your skis also limits your ability to balance on the frictionless surface of the snow. The other common mistake skiers will make at this level is misplacing or throwing their shoulders. It's not clear to me if this is a natural instinct, or if it's a learned habit due to how we've been practicing skiing up until this point. When we were practicing in our earlier lessons, our chest was often facing laterally to the fall line (as opposed to facing downhill). This is fine for things like traversal, sidestepping, or sideslipping. However, we need to be keeping our chest facing downhill when linking turns together, which is the proper shoulder placement for skiers at this stage of development. If you take a moment to twist your chest left and right while skiing, you can observe how your shoulders can help guide the rest of your body (and by extension the skis). Your upper body affects what is happening in your lower body, which is primarily what guides our skis.

Let's break the concept of shoulder placement down a little further. When completing a C-turn, a skier's shoulders will likely shift so that the chest is horizontal across the fall line (as they would in a traversal). When a skier resists that shoulder rotation and keeps their chest downhill while skiing, it helps the body embrace that forward-leaning skiing stance. This is one tip that can help skiers turn on demand, which is the goal of practicing S-turns. Paying attention to what your shoulders are doing can help you overcome the instinct to resist downhill motion, putting you in a better position to guide the skis.

Another tip that will help skiers adopt the right ski posture, and thus help them maintain control while practicing S-turns, is to pay attention to what the hands are doing. You should be keeping your hands in front of you, facing the bottom of the hill even as you turn. This tip can also help to correct shoulder position, enabling a skiing stance that will benefit a skier's overall performance. This also puts your poles in the right position to initiate turns, which is one advantage of using poles for skiing. When the pole is planted in front of a skier, it subconsciously helps some people embrace a proper skiing stance. This means that skiers who are using their poles correctly are bobbing or squatting slightly forward every time they plant their poles in front of them, helping them embrace the ideal skiing posture to turn on command. A proper pole plant is just a flick of the wrist, so that your hands stay in front while the pole tip moves back into a normal skiing position. You might notice that this prepares you for the next pole plant, meaning S-turns can become narrower and tighter.

When I'm teaching lessons, I often have to repeat myself in order for the lessons to be absorbed. As many teachers can attest, the challenge in teaching is that the teacher must explain the same concept in several ways until the message is understood. I've said this many times, but it's worth repeating because of how important the concept is for those seeking to progress in this sport. Leaning backwards or resisting that downhill acceleration will only make controlling your skis more difficult. If you're struggling to turn your C-turns into S-turns because you're leaning back, I have a few more tricks that can help students internalize this concept.

One suggestion I might mention in my lessons is to try squatting slightly, which lowers a skier's center of gravity. This adjustment can make some skiers feel more stable, which can help their confidence when initiating turns. Another helpful recommendation is to try bouncing on the tips of the toes throughout every turn. This motion is helpful because the motion puts a skier's weight slightly forward and transfers kinetic energy into the skis, allowing the skier to gain a greater sense of control over their skis.

While leaning back is what tends to get beginners in trouble, there are exceptions where leaning back can be beneficial. For example, in deep snow you can lean back to help rise to the surface of fresh powder. In deep powder you can also reliably initiate turns when leaning further back than you normally would. Because beginners tend to learn on groomed or compact snow, the emphasis should generally be forward on your skis to guide turns. Even when leaning back can be beneficial, you never want to be leaning back so much that you aren't prepared to get into an athletic skiing position at a moment's notice.

For movie fans, there is one more tip that might help you visualize how to progress into an expert skier. You've probably heard of Pixar, the famous animation studio that consistently produces some of the most critically acclaimed movies in cinema history. One such movie was called *The Incredibles*, and I would find it incredibly unbelievable if you've never seen it. While it might seem silly to bring this up, in the movie there is a character voiced by Samuel Jackson called "Frozone." If you recall, Samual Jackson's character uses his superhero ice powers to speed-skate across the city. The reason I bring this character up, besides being iconic and easily recognizable, is that the motion he uses to speed-skate is the exact same motion that enables skiers to turn on even the steepest terrain. While it's true he is technically ice skating, the motions Frozone uses are very similar to the motions a skier uses while racing or when skiing steep terrain. The key difference is that as skiers we only want to emulate his upper body, and our legs won't be nearly as animated or active. Sometimes students need a visual reference like this for the knowledge to sink in, and Frozone is a good visual representation of how we maintain control on snow and ice. As you might remember from the movie, Frozone has an extremely pronounced forward posture while keeping his hands forward to maintain his course. The constant hand swinging he does can also be beneficial for turning on skis, although it does run the risk of teaching students to throw their shoulders. That being said, as long as you keep your shoulders pointing downhill you can actually throw your hands forward as Frozone does in the movies. You may notice that the added forward motion of the hands allows you to turn whenever you feel like it. The only difference between an expert skier and Frozone is that skiers don't have to push off the ground with their legs like an ice skater does. Aside from that, and the fact that Frozone's posture is comically overemphasized, the similarities are striking. To keep the

Disney theme going, you can keep fueling yourself with motivating phrases like "I am speed," or "ka-chow!"

Some common issues skiers might run into at this stage is the skis are sometimes crossing or catching sudden edges. If you're having problems with your skis crossing, make sure that you aren't relying on the pizza wedge method. Sometimes those inner edges will get away from you when using the inside edges to lead turns, which can lead to skis crossing over each other. If you're frequently catching an edge, it might be that you're overemphasizing the ski's edges or using the wrong edges for the situation. Remember that the goal is to use the ski's edges to carve *with* the snow, not against it. Turning should be a smooth motion that doesn't need to be excessively forced. These issues can also be caused by equipment issues, so make sure that your boots, skis, and bindings are all attached securely and working properly. Check the edges of your skis as well, as rough or jagged edges could lead to inconsistent maneuverability.

If you're still struggling with the S-turns, the problem might be that you aren't fully comfortable with C-turns. It might be worth revisiting previous drills on a smaller hill to get more comfortable with the fundamentals. For most skiers who are struggling to link their C-turns into S-turns, the issue is a lack of confidence. A reliance on the pizza wedge technique or an improper skiing stance are two signs that a skier isn't confident initiating S-turns. In this transition period where skiers are learning to link turns together, it can be helpful to try taking wider turns to reduce speed and regain a sense of control. Once you're comfortable making these wider S-shaped turns without stopping, initiating turns on demand will become easier. With enough practice and experience, S-turns will become narrower as confidence in turn initiation grows.

Power sliding is an advanced skill used by skiers to stop as quickly as possible. Whether a student realizes it or not, they've already had some practice utilizing the mechanics behind this technique. The motions used for sideslipping are nearly identical to the motions a skier uses to power slide. The challenge lies in transitioning from a turn into the sudden stopping motion used to halt a sideslip. Being able to stop rapidly is incredibly important, which is why learning how to power slide becomes crucial as skiers become more comfortable with faster speeds and steeper terrain. Once a skier can consistently complete S-turns, it's time to truly master this skill.

It's almost impossible to power slide using the pizza wedge turning method. To practice power slides, gather some speed and initiate a few proper turns. Once you have reached a controlled riding speed, end the final turn with the stopping motion used for a sideslip. This will require the skis to be positioned laterally to the hill. The goal of this drill is not to slip sideways at all, it's to engage the uphill edges of the ski into the snow as forcefully and quickly as possible. Bend the knees and shift your weight into the uphill edges. As long as you are leaning uphill into the ski's uphill edges, your downhill edges should not catch and cause you to crash. Since a full C-turn puts your skis more laterally to the fall line, applying your edges at the end of the turn acts as a brake to halt progress quickly. Whether that's at the end of a turn or while sideslipping, there's no difference in how the edges are being used. A turn can become a sudden stop once the skier understands how to combine the guiding edge control skills used for turning and the forceful edge control skills used for halting a sideslip.

One trick that can help skiers who are struggling to initiate a power slide is to try a "hopping" motion while rotating the body sideways to the fall line, landing on the uphill edges of the skis. This is a good test of edge awareness, because "hopping to a stop" will either work immediately or fail disastrously. If you catch an edge after hopping sideways to stop, it means that your skis are angled too far downhill. Hopping into a power slide forces a skier to apply the correct edges while testing edge control and balance. While hopping into a power slide is a good test of edge awareness, it isn't a technique that's reliable enough to replace a true power slide. Keep practicing until you can consistently power slide at the end of a C-turn without hopping. You'll soon be an expert at this advanced braking technique.

It may take quite some time to master these skills, but once a skier is comfortable applying all of the previous techniques they will have become a certified intermediate-level skier. Once a skier progresses past this point, they should still stick to terrain within their ability level. That said, skiers who have internalized these skills should have the ability to gradually start conquering more difficult terrain. For skiers who feel they don't have full control, don't be afraid to revisit previous lessons or find more manageable runs to practice on. For those that have come this far, progression is largely up to your personal level of comfort applying the fundamentals in more challenging terrain.

If you do begin to attempt expert runs, be aware that the conditions will drastically change what is considered feasible or safe. If the conditions are icier than usual, for example, it may not be wise to attempt more difficult ski runs. Even experts avoid skiing expert terrain when conditions are icy or if there is not enough fresh snow to navigate safely. The other route a skier's progression could follow might focus on tricks, which would lead students to practicing skills like skiing backwards or doing jumps. In the next stage of progression, we'll discuss the more advanced stages of learning.

STAGE 4: JUMPING, TRICKS, AND DEVELOPING EXPERTISE

How do you teach a ski student to be the next Lindsey Vonn? That's like asking how you'd teach a basketball player to be the next LeBron James. While instructors can provide a foundation of helpful skills, there are limitations to the level of skill ski students can achieve solely through coaching.

One thing that will take your abilities to the next level is practice. It seems like a cop out to mention this, as it seems like that would be common sense. However, skiing is a remarkably niche and novel sport. Due to the novelty of skiing, common sense might not be a common revelation. Think about your favorite professional athlete and how much dedication they have for their sport. How many three-point shots do you think that Stephen Curry has practiced over his career? He's done it so many times that he can shoot a three-pointer blindfolded. It's no different with skiing, and there's no substitute for practicing the movements. For most skiers, skiing is a hobby or a sport they'll engage with a few times a year. Yet a high level of mastery as a skier requires dedication, hundreds (or thousands) of hours of practice, and familiarity with the motions. Some people are lucky enough to have access to ski slopes year-round, and these people who accumulate countless hours of practice are inevitably the ones that make a name for themselves in this sport.

When it comes to **skiing expert terrain,** practice is what makes perfect. You have to have practiced the fundamentals enough times that you can initiate your turns on command, stop on command, and maintain the proper athletic stance regardless of the steepness of a hill. I can offer tips to point a skier in the right direction, but adopting those lessons and ingraining them into your muscle memory takes dedication. That said, there are a few additional tips I can provide that can help an intermediate-level skier become an expert. Let's quickly revisit the fundamentals and troubleshoot some of the problems that could be holding a skier back in steep or difficult terrain.

While leaning back is typically the most common balancing error students have on steep slopes, it's possible that something else is causing issues. The positioning of your skis is one example, and a person's skis should be no wider than shoulder width apart while skiing. The position of the skis will preferably be closer together than shoulder width, with the skier's weight distributed evenly on both skis.

Another issue skiers might have when encountering steep terrain is being too far forward. This is a somewhat issue due to how uncomfortable this overemphasized forward-leaning position is, in addition to how bizarre this stance looks. You'll know when a skier is too far forward if their knees are locked straight, or if the waist is bent to an extremely awkward degree. A skier should never lock their knees or extend their legs completely straight, as a slight bend in the knees is required to absorb impacts and change direction on command. It's much more common for skiers to be leaning too far back, but we've discussed this issue numerous times and it's not worth discussing further.

Another issue that might be holding skiers back in extreme terrain is their edge control. If a skier is crossing their skis frequently or catching edges that throw them off balance, the problem is likely due to an incorrect usage of the ski's edges. Crossing skis happens when the skis are angled in different directions. It's bound to happen if one edge is being emphasized more than the other, or if a skier is using the pizza wedge technique to turn. This can also be a sign of equipment issues. Check to see that the ski's edges are sharpened. Additionally, ensure that all equipment is securely tightened with no wiggle movement in the boots, bindings, or skis. Loose equipment is dangerous and makes controlling the skis more difficult. If your ski equipment is functioning properly and you're still crossing skis, look down at your feet while skiing to make sure that the skis are matching and moving predictably when initiating turns.

Leg strength can also be a common issue for skiers at any level, as the muscles used for skiing might be ones that don't see much use in normal daily life. While this is yet another reason why practice helps skiers progress, there are things you can do to improve your leg strength and be better equipped for your next ski session. Squats, lunges, glute exercises, flexibility training, and even ab workouts (particularly lower ab groups) are some beneficial exercises that strengthen the muscle groups primarily used for skiing. Squats and lunges in particular can be especially helpful. Squats will help skiers practice the motion needed to recover from turns, while also helping skiers hold a proper skiing stance for long periods of time. Lunges will help skiers hold matching ski positions and regain the ideal skiing stance whenever the skis drift apart.

Another common problem that skiers develop on steeper inclines is a tendency to throw their shoulders. This is a similar problem to leaning too far back on the skis, because it's a sign the terrain is too steep for comfort. To overcome their fears, skiers will often swing their shoulders to ensure they carry enough initial movement to complete a turn. They'll also tend to point their shoulders laterally across the hill, instead of having their hands and shoulders facing forward downhill (which helps a skier prepare for turn after turn). There are a few things you can do to rectify this and learn better skiing habits. First, move to a comfortable slope that's within your abilities. Next, flip your ski poles upside down and hold them in front of you while crossing them into an "X." Point the center of this X-shaped crosshair towards an object at the bottom of the hill. Keep the center focused on the object as you ski downhill. Adopting this position forces a skier to keep their hands in front of them while their shoulders are pointed downhill. While it seems like a gimmick, this drill helps develop a skier's muscle memory when verbal instruction is not enough. It's a drill that ensures students are using a more functional ski stance, and will help them maintain control of their turns as they transition to steeper terrain.

As I alluded to at the start of this section, expertise isn't something that can be taught. Expertise is earned, generally through countless hours of practice. While there are some exceptional athletes who have a knack for skiing, there's no shortcuts or magic words I can share to replace the learned experience that comes from dedicating yourself to the sport. If you continue to stick with the sport, there's no doubt in my mind that you'll reach the goals you've set for yourself. It might not happen overnight, but with enough time you will become the expert skier you've always dreamed of becoming.

While skiing expert terrain will be a goal for some skiers, other skiers may choose to focus on practicing **stunts or jumps**. A good foundation for this type of skiing can be practiced in the off-season summer months, where skiers can develop their "wings" by learning tricks on a trampoline, utilizing foam pits designed for extreme sports, or by jumping into pools of water. This type of practice teaches important concepts that are difficult to teach, such as acrobatic awareness and controlling rotations while midair. For those of you who practice flips and spins, you might notice that extending your limbs slows rotations down. Tucking your arms and legs in does the opposite, speeding rotations up significantly.

At this point, we're not really talking about skiing anymore. These are acrobatic skills that are related to gymnastics, instead of the technical skiing skills we've been discussing previously. This is why it's a good idea to learn acrobatic skills before attempting stunts on skis. When you're on the snow there is often less room for error, so fundamental skills in both gymnastics and skiing should ideally be strong before you combine them.

If you feel like you're ready to start hitting jumps on your skis, make sure to practice on smaller jumps before working up to larger ones. When jumping on skis, keep your skis centered and push off the ground evenly with both feet just before the crest of the jump. This gives you more control and prevents you from being passively rotated by the angle of the jump. When landing a jump, remember to keep your knees bent and angle the skis to match the landing. Landing on the snow can be forgiving when it's fresh or deep, but generally jumps and landings are made of compact snow. This is why your landing zone should ideally have a downhill slope. A downhill landing minimizes resistance to a skier's velocity, thereby reducing the impact forces upon landing. Landing on flat ground, or God forbid an uphill landing, can be devastating to the connective tissue in your joints.

Something that can help you land more jumps is to "stomp the landing." Stomping the landing is a technique that utilizes a ski's flexibility to help absorb the impact of jumps. The tail-ends of your skis can be used to absorb impacts like a leaf spring. To stomp the landing, extend (or "stomp") your feet down into the snow while landing a jump. Be sure to land with your knees slightly bent, as you don't want to overextend your stomp to the point where your knees pop out of their sockets or snap from the force of the landing. If done correctly the tail-end of your skis will bend and absorb the impact, which transfers kinetic energy forward instead of directing that force into your body. In addition to absorbing the impact forces of a jump, the forward force transferred into your skis can help guide them in the right direction to increase stability after landing. Your skis can also be pre-loaded to help boost into the air like a springboard. Manipulating the skis in this way takes a rider's abilities to the next level. You can pre-load your skis by transferring your weight into your ski tips or tail-ends, which provides flair or extra height to jumps.

After getting comfortable jumping and landing on small jumps, you can eventually start to attempt larger jumps. From there, it's a fairly self-explanatory process to start grabbing your skis midair. To perform **grab tricks**, the best advice I can give is to practice stretching so that you're flexible enough for midair flair. If you're feeling bold, you can extend your legs while grabbing to perform a "tweaked" grab. These grabs require more airtime, but they also add a ton of style points to any trick!

Riding switch is the act of skiing backwards. Riding switch is a skill that can be practiced once a skier is familiar with fundamental turning techniques. Skiing backwards is similar to normal skiing, all it takes is a slight tilt of the knees to guide the skis and change direction. You'll need to partially squat in order to shift your weight downhill, slightly bending the knees to keep your body weight over the leading edges. In this situation, the leading edges are towards the tail-end of your skis. A helpful tip for skiers practicing this skill is to look over a shoulder to guide turns. Looking over your shoulders will not only help you see what's downhill, it will also help accentuate your edges as the weight of your upper body shifts from side to side. Looking over your left shoulder puts slightly more weight over your left edges, which turns you to the left. If you want to turn right while riding switch, just turn your head and look over your right shoulder. This concept can get a little confusing when looking over your shoulder, as your left edges appear to be on the right relative to your vision when looking backward. Don't get too mixed up on the specifics, just feel it out and the motions will become more natural.

Butters are another fun trick to practice at this stage of progression. "Butters" are essentially just wheelies on skis. You can "wheelie" off the nose-end or tail-end tips of your skis to add style or show off your balancing skills. It's simple to explain but hard to master. Just keep your knees slightly bent, emphasize an excessive forwards or backwards lean while skiing, and pray for good results! Some flexibility training and an ability to balance will go a long way towards achieving good results.

You can also begin to incorporate some **spins or flips** into your jumps. When spinning, keep your shoulders facing forward while taking off from a jump. After that, you can guide your rotations by rotating your shoulders in the direction you want to spin. Landing these types of rotations is easier said than done, but generally people recommend

136

pointing your chest at the landing as soon as you spot it. This helps you put your legs where they need to be by the time you reach the ground. The advice is similar when it comes to flips, although you may need to tuck your legs tight to your chest to aid the rotation. Since tucking in your limbs speeds up rotations, you'll need to extend your legs towards the end of your flip to slow down rotation speed and brace for landing. As always, make sure that your knees are slightly bent when landing jumps to prevent injury.

Grinding is another expert-level skill that not all skiers will develop. Boxes and rails are common features you'll see at a ski resort's terrain park. These hard surfaces should only be ridden if you're wearing a helmet. Even with the adequate safety equipment, there is little room for error while grinding. Features such as these are unforgiving in the event of a crash. For skiers who are interested in grinding, I'll provide a few pointers that may help. Grinding requires impeccable balance and the highest levels of edge awareness. Any mistake can quickly lead to catching an edge, or a sudden imbalance that could lead to a wipeout. Some skiers prefer to detune their edges when practicing their grinds. Detuning your skis requires you to round your edges instead of keeping them at a sharp 90-degree angle. Detuning the entire length of your skis will obviously limit your ability to carve and turn, so if you go this route you'll have to be very careful about what sections of your skis you choose to detune for grinding. Some skiers will detune the portions of their skis they grind with, keeping the leading edges sharp for turning purposes. Some skiers don't detune their edges at all, which means they have to be extra careful when grinding.

When it comes to practicing grinds, start by practicing on boxes. Boxes are much wider and easier to balance on than rails or pipes, so boxes are generally considered to be a good starting point. Lowering your center of gravity by squatting down slightly can provide added balance and helps keep you centered during the length of a grind. Try not to panic if you begin to rotate accidentally, as attempting to overcorrect may cause you to become unbalanced or catch an edge. Instead, embrace the rotation or look for an opportunity to safely dismount. Once you are comfortable with boxes you can move onto rails, which are often more difficult for skiers due to the smaller surface area being balanced on. The advice for grinding rails is similar to grinding boxes, just keep your weight over your feet and try to keep your balance perfectly centered. If the rail gets away from under your feet, it's usually safer to dismount instead of attempting to correct.

The level of expertise you'll be able to achieve as a skier will depend on many factors. Professional skiers practice their skills year round, both on and off the snow. You likely don't need that level of dedication to meet your goals as a skier, so your progression at this stage will entirely depend on what you want to gain from this sport. Not everyone's goal is to become the next Olympic-level competitive skier, so learning how to do double backflips is not something I feel is worth discussing for the purpose of this book.

It's my belief that all skiers have a shared goal. Our shared goal isn't to land a double backflip, it's to have fun. That's why the final stage of progression I teach is how to have fun. You might be asking, "Why isn't this the first stage of progression?" It's a fair question with a simple answer. Over my years of teaching, I've found that many students have a goal in their minds to build towards the final stage of progression as quickly as possible. This mindset is problematic and leads to potentially dangerous situations. By placing enjoyment at the peak level of accomplishment, students subconsciously focus on having fun at every stage of development. Having fun should be the ultimate goal for every skier, regardless of their skill or current stage of progression.

STAGE 5: HAVING FUN

Having fun is the ultimate objective for a developing skier throughout every stage of development. If you had to choose between becoming a professional skier who hated skiing or a beginner-level rider who was enjoying every moment on the snow, which person would you rather be? I think the best answer, and the answer that most rational people would pick, is to be the person who enjoys skiing.

Every skier has encountered their share of challenges while progressing in this sport. Despite the challenges, the falls, and the fails, they chose to pick themselves up and keep trying. Every rider on the mountain has experienced difficulties, and we kept coming back to winter sports because we enjoy them. This universal experience is something that all riders have in common. It's one of the reasons why mountain communities are special.

This is why having fun is the final stage of progression. It's the goal every skier should be aiming for throughout their development. I've played a lot of sports over the years, but I haven't enjoyed all of them. Having fun is what makes this sport so special. What's the point of skiing if you're not enjoying it?

There are lots of things you can do to keep the experience fresh as you become more advanced. You might want to share this sport with friends, family, or the world (as I do with my ski and snowboard books). You might choose to adopt the skiing lifestyle or culture that fosters a healthy mountain community. You might apply what you've learned to push the sport forward in a way that's new, innovative, or rewarding. You might begin to search for the most pristine conditions and the freshest powder, knowing that few people on this planet will experience something so magical. Or you could pioneer original goals for yourself, reviving the learning and growth process you faced as a first-time skier. Don't be afraid to mix things up either. Have a snowball fight, take breaks, make some snow art, enjoy the views, and live in the moment.

At some point, each bird has to leave the nest and fly on their own. That's the beauty of a sport like skiing, it's up to you to decide when your next adventure begins. Having fun with the sport means there is no pressure to conquer a specific obstacle or goal. It's your responsibility to invent new ways to have fun while progressing at your own pace. After you've mastered the basics of skiing, the sky's the limit.

My job is simply to teach you about good habits, suggest proper techniques, provide a few incentives, and offer some important safety tips. It's your job to implement those lessons and have fun while doing it. In the following chapters, I'll provide you additional safety tips and other miscellaneous insights that might help you maximize your enjoyment while skiing. That being said, skiers who are enjoying their time skiing have already succeeded. This stage of development, the one that focuses on fun, is the true mark of a skier. Skiers who are having fun are performing at the highest levels possible.

7 HOW TO SKI (CROSS-COUNTRY SKIING)

Cross-country skiing is a type of skiing that makes it easy to travel large distances on snow. It is considered a recreational sport in the same way that downhill skiing is, however, cross-country skiing has some key differences. Since cross-country ski bindings allow a skier's heels to swivel, motions like turning are limited and achieved with slightly different actions. Although cross-country skiing is an excellent method of transportation, it doesn't have the same reputation for downhill performance as downhill skis do.

I'm not going to go into as much detail in terms of lesson progression when it comes to cross-country skiing, as many of the same concepts previously discussed will apply to cross-country skiing. Instead, I'll cover the key differences and provide a few tips to help people who are interested in this type of skiing.

Although downhill skiing and cross-country skiing have some similarities, the detached heel of a cross-country ski binding does complicate things. One of the major differences is that cross-country skis require a different method of turning. While I emphasized the importance of a forward-leaning stance when downhill skiing, the detachable heel means that leaning too far forward will imbalance a cross-country skier and lead to a crash. Instead, you'll want to be centered on your skis throughout a turn. It can be helpful to lower your center of gravity by dropping a knee while turning, similar to a lunge exercise. This stance can help a cross-country skier maintain balance and effectively turn.

This lunging motion is what's known as a "drop turn." Due to the unique bindings of a cross-country ski, these drop turns are an advanced type of turn that only cross-country skiers can execute. Drop turning allows a skier to lower their center of gravity, and increases stability through a downhill turn. The disadvantage of this type of turn is that it takes a significant amount of strength to consistently initiate or hold, and is a little unreliable if improperly performed.

It might be a good idea to use slightly longer poles when cross-country skiing, since you'll often be using them from an upright stance. Duck walking is an effective way to propel forward on cross-country skis as well, and many of the strategies for traversing are applicable to both types of skiing. Cross-country skiers might want to consider investing in a pair of "skins," which are optional pieces of equipment used to push skis forward and assist with things like ascending hills. Ski skins, or Nordic ski skins, are usually made of mohair or nylon. They are installed or removed easily, and cover a ski's base to provide traction without restricting forward movement. You can install ski skins on downhill skis as well, but they are much more effective when paired with cross-country skis due to their travel-focused design.

Kick gliding and skating are two ways cross-country skiers propel forward on flat ground or up hills. Skating is when you push off your side edges, similar to an ice skater.

Generally speaking, shorter skis are preferred for cross-country skiers who rely on skating. Kick gliding is unique to cross-country skiing. To kick glide, the skis stay parallel as the skier walks forward by "kicking" or lunging each leg forward. This motion allows the skier to glide forward, and kick gliding is especially effective when using skins.

Many of the things that cross-country skis excel at should come fairly naturally. Sliding, gliding, and trekking through the snow are all things that most skiers can adapt to quickly. Especially for skiers who understand the fundamentals of edge control and basic ski movements on snow, learning how to cross-country ski should be no problem. Because of the relative ease of transportation and movement on snow, cross-country skiing is an excellent exercise option for people who are interested in adventuring across long distances in snowy climates.

Cross-country bindings and hybrid cross-country bindings allow skiers to access more of the mountain and specialize their style of skiing. Unlike downhill skis that only enable freestyle or backcountry skiing opportunities, the different types of skiing available to cross-country skiers include these styles and expand on them. Telemark skiing is nearly identical to cross-country skiing, but covers steeper slopes than the rolling terrain a cross-country skier would normally encounter. Telemark skiers use stronger gear to make downhill sections easier and safer. Alpine touring is a type of skiing that requires more exploration, going beyond the territory a backcountry skier could feasibly reach using downhill ski bindings. Mountaineering goes beyond what this book covers, and it involves the use of climbing gear to scale and explore everything a skier could possibly encounter on the mountain.

While all skiers should be aware of the potential hazards of the sport, cross-country skiers are typically seeking to explore through unexplored terrain. They may be inclined to move beyond the boundaries of the ski resort. For this reason, cross-country skiers should aim to become knowledgeable about the potential hazards and prepare appropriately.

8   Snow Conditions

Did you know that the Swedish language has at least twenty-five different words for snow? The English language lacks many of these terms used to describe different qualities of snow. You can see how "slush" does not describe the snow we typically picture falling from the sky, and why detailing these differences sometimes becomes necessary. These subtle, or sometimes not so subtle, differences in snow can impact a person's skiing in various ways.

Snow conditions can change quickly, and some snow conditions are more ideal than others. The current snow conditions are an important consideration for skiers. Even expert skiers will avoid difficult terrain when the conditions are bad.

The snow conditions that affect skiing are called fresh snow, compact snow, crud, ice, and melting snow (sometimes called spring snow). Fresh snow provides a consistently smooth riding surface and can cushion crashes depending on the depth. Spring snow is slushy and fairly forgiving. Compact snow also provides a good riding surface, but is less forgiving to skiers who crash on it. Ice is unforgiving, dangerous, and as hard as cement. Crud is snow mixed with clumps or patches of ice. Being knowledgeable about these various snow conditions will benefit skiers by helping them adapt faster and avoid taking unnecessary risks.

FRESH SNOW

Snow has unique qualities when it's fresh. Fresh snow is what skiers commonly refer to as "powder," a pillowy layer of snow that cushions falls and provides a consistent riding surface. Fresh snow is universally considered by experienced skiers to be the most ideal riding conditions due to these qualities, with dry snow being the most favorable due to its tendency to resist compacting. You can tell if snow is dry when it doesn't hold shape when trying to pack a snowball, whereas wet snow that forms a snowball easily will pack down and is easily tracked out. Wet snow also doesn't feel as airy underfoot while skiing and can bog skiers down more than dry snow. Regardless of whether the snow is wet or dry, fresh snow is extremely fun to ride on.

Of course, a significant amount of snowfall is needed to truly be considered fresh snow conditions. For example, an inch of snow on top of a sheet of ice wouldn't provide the same consistency or benefits that deep snow would. You can generally push your ability level in fresh powder, since the deep snow acts like an airbag in the event of a crash.

Skiing on fresh powder requires a slightly different approach. Skiers need to be a little further back on their skis than normal, which helps the ski's tips rise above the surface and stay afloat. Luckily, you shouldn't have too much trouble skiing in fresh powder once you get the hang of this difference. Initiating turns is usually easier and feels more natural in powder compared to skiing on compact snow or ice. If you're leaning slightly back but still having trouble skiing in fresh snow, it could be that your bindings are set too far forward. Another issue may be that your skis perform poorly in powder, which could be due to their shape or design. A fresh application of wax can solve some of these issues by helping skiers maintain higher speeds, which reduces the chances of sinking.

Skiers can typically handle more difficult terrain than they normally would in deep snow, because turning will slow you down more than usual. There is also more room for error due to the forgiving nature of powder. That being said, you might need to gain more speed than you are comfortable with in order to stay afloat. Skiing fresh powder can also be more demanding, requiring a significant amount of leg strength. It's a good idea to stick near the trails and stay higher up on a slope when skiing in powder. This reduces the chance a skier will be stalled and have to hike out of low spots or flat sections.

This leads us to the dangers of deep snow, which are unique compared to other snow conditions. If the snow depth is deep enough, it can be easy for skiers to become stuck or buried. At best this can be frustrating, and at worst this can become a life-threatening situation. Deep snow can behave like quicksand, and the only way to resurface is by packing down a platform to stand on without sinking. If you do become stuck, you can use your skis to pack a wider area of snow down as you attempt to work your way up to the surface (somewhat like building a staircase). If you crash and are buried under the snow, you should try your best to get your head above your feet. Be careful if you detach your skis, as it's easier to sink in deep snow when your skis are unattached. Due to the added risk of becoming buried, it's a good idea to ski with other people you trust when riding in extremely deep snow.

Deep snow can also create pockets around trees, which are known as tree wells. When tree branches block enough falling snow, a void is formed that can easily collapse or trap skiers who get too close. Since not all trees will form tree wells, tree wells can lull skiers into a false sense of security. It's a good idea to avoid skiing near trees, as tree wells can be unpredictable. Fresh snow can also increase the likelihood of avalanches, although it is not the only snow condition where avalanches can occur. We'll talk about these hazards later on. For now, just remember that tree wells, avalanches, and becoming stuck in the snow are potential dangers in fresh snow conditions.

While deep snow can be challenging at first, fresh powder will likely be your favorite snow condition once you have mastered the fundamentals of skiing on more compact snow surfaces. When fresh powder becomes tracked out or compressed, it creates the snow condition known as compact snow. But before we talk about compact snow, let's discuss another highly favorable snow condition.

Spring Snow Conditions (Melting Snow)

Spring snow conditions are slushy, wet, and surprisingly forgiving in a crash. You can expect this type of snow in spring, when compacted snow begins to soften up and melt. Melting snow behaves almost like fresh powder, albeit much thicker and denser. Many of the same rules for powder apply, however, you'll have to stay on your toes while skiing since spring snow is heavier and more compact than fresh snow.

There is one major downside to spring snow conditions, and that is that the snow tends to eat through wax and clings to the skis. If your skis aren't sufficiently waxed you'll notice the snow randomly "grabs" at your skis, slowing you down at an uncomfortably fast rate. Luckily this is an easy fix, either through your regular maintenance with hot wax or with additional applications of rub-on wax applied throughout the day as needed. Since spring conditions eat through wax quickly, I recommend using natural or non-toxic waxes to avoid handling waxes with harmful PFAS more than necessary. I use a natural rub-on wax throughout spring that is not only safe to handle, but is also more effective and longer-lasting than fluorinated waxes.

As long as you are staying in the sunshine, spring snow conditions stay soft throughout the day. That being said, you can't get away with leaning back as much as you would in powder conditions. Be aware that shaded areas can remain icy, so don't expect the most consistent riding surfaces. Even snowy surfaces that were starting to melt can quickly refreeze as soon as the sun's energy stops reaching it.

Another thing to remember about spring conditions is that snowy rooftops are melting as well, cascading snow on unsuspecting victims below. While you never want to linger underneath buildings with snow or icicles on them, the frequency of rooftops "shedding" their snow or ice increases in warmer weather. You've been warned!

COMPACT SNOW

Compact snow is probably the most common snow condition you'll find at a ski resort. Fresh snow will either be compacted by other riders or by snow grooming machinery, and nearly every ski resort will make a significant effort to provide groomed runs. Compacted and groomed snow provides a uniform surface for reliable riding. Compact snow is enjoyable and consistent to ski on, but it can also be less forgiving in the event of a crash.

While a skier can get away with leaning slightly back in deeper snow, leaning back can throw off your balance and limit your turning capabilities on compact snow. Most skiers will learn how to ski on compact snow, which is why I emphasize the importance of being further forward on your skis to initiate your edges and turn. While compact snow is less forgiving than fresh snow, learning how to ski on compacted snow will provide you a great foundation to understand important skiing concepts.

CRUD (MIXED ICE AND SNOW)

Crud is a rough mixture of ice chunks and snow. While it's possible to ski in cruddy snow conditions, you need to actively avoid large ice chunks that could be problematic. Your skis can sometimes bust through crud without issues, but larger chunks of ice are rigid and will throw you off your skis if you hit them. Mixed ice and snow can be an unpredictable riding surface, which means it's an exceptionally dangerous riding surface. Due to the unpredictability of cruddy snow, these conditions are as dangerous (if not more dangerous) than skiing on ice alone.

Cruddy snow conditions can limit the types of runs you are able to ski down. For example, an expert skier might avoid steeper runs in cruddy conditions to avoid a potential crash. I'd recommend limiting yourself to fully compacted groomed runs when the snow conditions are cruddy. If you do find yourself skiing through crud, stay on your toes and be ready for any surprises.

ICE

Icy conditions are generally disadvantageous for skiers, except for speed skiers who prefer intentionally frozen racecourses. These conditions are fast and unforgiving. Crashing on ice is one of the most dangerous situations you can encounter as a skier, and falling onto ice at skiing speeds is like smacking into the pavement on a bicycle. Since ice is nearly frictionless, crashing on ice also increases the chances of an uncontrolled slide.

If you do happen to crash or slide uncontrollably on ice, do whatever you can to point your feet downhill and engage your edges. Even if you lose a ski, your ski boots can be used like ski edges, potentially providing enough traction to regain control and stop sliding. Stopping yourself with anything but a hard edge is practically impossible on ice, so forcing your feet (and by extension your edges) into the ice is pretty much the only option you have to slow down.

Steeper courses that you could reasonably manage in powder may be impossible to ski down safely in icy conditions, as the rigid nature of ice makes carving turns more difficult and can easily throw a skier off balance if the ice forms unevenly. For most skiers at the highest levels of this sport, the goal isn't to conquer icy conditions but to avoid them in favor of better snow conditions. Put simply, ice is much more dangerous to ride on than snow.

Sometimes it's not possible to avoid icy surfaces, so it's good to learn how to ski through icy patches. Keep your weight forward and be ready to carve a turn into the ice. The motion is very similar to how turns are initiated on compact snow, although you might have to put more effort into this forward motion than you normally would to engage the edges of your skis. Edge awareness and edge control is very important when it comes to skiing on ice. You can visualize an ice skater's movements to help visualize how skiing is done on icy surfaces, because comparing the sports is practically identical in icy conditions. The main difference is that more effort is needed to carve turns into ice on skis, whereas the blades of an ice skate carve into the ice constantly. Since skis aren't as effective at carving into ice, icy conditions are not ideal.

Knowing the different types of snow conditions will help you stay safe on the mountain. Keep in mind that snow conditions can change quickly, and different sections of a run can have different conditions as well. If you were thinking about attempting to ski steep terrain, knowing that there was only an inch of fresh snow on top of a layer of ice might help you evaluate the potential risks. Even experts might think twice if this was the case, as the layer of ice could easily become exposed. Understanding the differences of various snow conditions will help you plan safe routes, taking your expertise as a skier to the next level.

9 Navigating the Mountain

Ski resorts have a unique way of labeling a ski run's difficulty rating. Depending on what area of the world you are in, ski slopes will be labeled with shapes or colors (or both) to let riders know how challenging the upcoming terrain is. In this chapter we'll discuss the trail rating system, ski lifts, and other relevant tips to help skiers safely navigate the mountain.

Trail Difficulty Ratings Explained

Ski runs in the United States are labeled with green circles, blue squares, and black diamonds. The easiest ski runs are the green circles, where the angles of a slope are minimal with few or no obstacles on the course. Blue squares are runs that are slightly steeper. They may also include slightly more challenging sections or obstacles that make descending more difficult. Black diamond runs are steep and offer a significant challenge. This terrain should only be attempted by expert riders and may require ideal snow conditions to descend safely. Double black diamonds are reserved for the most dangerous courses. They can lead to steep chutes, cliffs, or other hazards that even expert skiers may struggle with. An orange oblong is used to label terrain parks, which are ski runs that contain ideal terrain for riders focusing on practicing jumps or tricks. They commonly contain kickers, tabletops, halfpipes, boxes, rails, and other unique features.

In other parts of the world, the trail difficulty rating system may just use colors. It's very similar to the trail rating system in the United States, with green circles and blue circles indicating the easiest runs. Red circles are more advanced runs, and black circles will mark the hardest runs at a ski resort. Regardless of where you are skiing, you should pay attention to the trail markers that indicate the difficulty of the ski runs ahead.

USING CHAIRLIFTS

Since most people learn how to ski at a ski resort, dedicated skiers will eventually need to learn how to ride a chairlift. Luckily, it's a fairly easy process. Newer chairlifts will slow down to comfortably and safely take riders to the top of a hill. Older chairlifts can be a bit trickier to board, but there are some tips that can make the process less intimidating. When it comes to loading onto chairlifts, the most important thing to remember is to keep your knees slightly bent while pointing your skis straight ahead.

If you've never used a chairlift, it might be useful to describe the loading process. The line for a chairlift will funnel into a waiting zone, and eventually a loading zone where the chairlift picks up small groups of riders. The etiquette for a chair lift is to wait your turn as you shuffle forward in line. If there are multiple lines, alternate groups from each line while doing your best to fill up each chairlift. This ensures everyone can get to the top of the mountain as efficiently as possible.

Once you're in line, move through the waiting zone until you can follow the next chair into the loading zone. Being able to use your poles can help you move through the lines easier, but if you are still having trouble moving around remember to use your edges (either by side stepping, utilizing a pizza wedge, or by duck walking). When you approach the loading zone, watch where the riders ahead of you are stopping to be picked up by the chairlift. When the group in front of you is being picked up, wait until their chairlift passes and you can follow behind it to wait for the next chair. Stop on the loading zone, which is where the riders ahead of you were picked up, and wait for your chairlift to reach you. You can either sit down once the chairlift reaches you while looking ahead, or you can look backwards over your shoulder while keeping your skis forward to grab the chair and help you sit down. For older chairlifts that don't slow down, looking backwards and grabbing the chair is the best way to safely seat yourself. If you're boarding an old two-seater chairlift with a pole in the middle of the chairlift, you'll want to grab said pole to make sure that it doesn't bonk into you while you're sitting down.

Once you sit down, hold your skis straight and keep your back flat to the seat. Some chairs will have an optional safety bar that can be pulled down, which is handy because chairlift seats can be icy or slick. If reaching for the safety bar feels unsafe, simply remain seated with your back flat. Enjoy the ride while you wait to unload.

Unloading a chairlift is a fairly simple process for skiers. When approaching the unloading area, make sure that the safety bar is up and raise the tips of your skis so they don't catch on the snow. Once your skis contact the snow, you should be able to stand up and ride away from the unloading zone. The best practice is to ski straight forward until you can maneuver away from the other riders exiting the chairlift. Don't stand in the way of the other skiers exiting the chairlift behind you. If you happen to fall, make an effort to quickly scoot away from the unloading zone. It's also a good idea to communicate with the other riders on your chairlift before unloading so that your paths don't cross while exiting.

OTHER TYPES OF LIFTS

While a chairlift is probably the most common type of lift you'll see, you might encounter other types of ski lifts. Some examples include gondolas, cable cars, funiculars, poma systems (sometimes called button lifts), t-bars, rope tows, and magic carpets. There are also helicopters, snowmobiles, and other various machines people can use instead of lifts, however, these are mostly utilized by advanced skiers and each topic could fill an entirely separate book. For this book, we'll only be covering the typical lifts you might encounter at a ski resort.

Gondolas are essentially chairlifts with added comfort, as they are enclosed with siding and doors to keep everyone inside shielded from the elements. They can fit larger groups of skiers at once, yet their bulky design means that they are prone to being shut down in bad weather. **Cable cars and funiculars** are also shielded from the elements, and they can transport even more riders than gondolas. Cable cars use a cable system, whereas funiculars operate on rails. When boarding for any of these lifts, you'll remove your skis and secure your equipment in the outer racks before stepping on board. Once you've stored your skis and poles, just walk onto the lift and wait to reach the top of the hill. Exiting the lift is a simple process, just grab your gear from the outer racks and go.

T-bars and poma systems are lifts that pull riders uphill while their skis are attached. Poma lifts have a button-shaped seat attached to the end of a bar. To use a poma, simply put the pole between your legs and keep your skis straight while traveling. When seated properly, the button-shaped seat will effortlessly pull you uphill as the lift moves forward. T-bars work the same way, the only difference being the seat area is stretched wide to pull two people at once. For either lift, store your poles under your armpit to keep your hands free and hold onto the lift. It's also important to keep your legs bent and skis straight to avoid catching any edges on the way up. The most difficult aspect of using these lifts are the initial moments of sudden acceleration. Some skiers find it's helpful to even out those initial forces by braking, although this is a somewhat risky strategy that can cause a crash. Even without braking, most riders should be able to glide uphill without much difficulty after a little practice.

Rope tows are usually the most unforgiving lifts you could find at a ski resort. While some rope tows have handles, you might see rope tows where skiers must physically grip a rope with all their strength to pull themselves uphill. Needless to say, using rope tows can often be more physically demanding than skiing itself. Skiers using a rope tow will need to store their poles under one armpit as they hold on, while simultaneously keeping their skis pointed straight. Instead of relying purely on hand strength, it might be helpful to put as much of your weight as possible down onto the rope as you hold on. Usually this is done by tucking the rope underneath your arm as you sit your weight down to further aid your grip. Many ski resorts have phased out or replaced rope tow lifts, as they are ineffective and obsolete compared to other lift systems. The ski area I live next to almost exclusively relies on rope tows, so if you ever visit Hurricane Ridge prepare for a rough day!

Magic carpets are an increasingly common type of lift. Despite their limitations, they are useful for beginners at the early stages of their development. They are essentially horizontal escalators that move riders uphill as they stand still. They're simple and easy to use. To board one, just ski into the loading zone and shuffle onto the "carpet" with your skis still attached. Since the carpet stays moving, it pulls skiers onto the track and takes them up to the top of the run. Stand firm and don't move around too much while you're riding up. To exit, just keep skiing forward. Beginners should have a lot of fun with these magic carpets, as they're simple lifts that allow riders to ski and use moving sidewalks at the same time! I'm not the only one who enjoys travelators, right?

SAFELY DESCENDING

Learning the fundamentals of skiing and paying attention to the trail difficulty ratings will go a long way towards helping skiers safely navigate the mountain. There are a few additional tips that will help you stay safe and have fun while skiing. Some of these tips can be applied regardless of where you're skiing, and are especially important for skiers who will be skiing outside of a resort.

Riding in a group is a safe way to practice skiing, assuming that your fellow riders are working together and communicating effectively. When skiing with others, one person can cautiously ride ahead to spot landings, check for hazards, and help the other group members avoid potential dangers. If an accident does occur, having other people nearby can speed up rescues or reduce first-aid response time. Your riding group can also signal others for help. The downside of riding with others is that some time will be wasted waiting for others in the group, but the numerous benefits far outweighs this mild inconvenience.

We talked about a few optional pieces of gear in earlier chapters, but for people skiing expert terrain or outside of a resort it's important to bring communication tools to stay in contact with fellow riders. Even a whistle can be a lifesaving tool in the event of an accident, so it's not a bad idea to include something like this with the rest of your skiing gear. Walkie-talkies are also useful devices for staying in communication with your fellow riders, as opposed to cell phones that might lack cell coverage (depending on your provider or where you're skiing). I know we've already discussed these optional pieces of equipment, but this gear shouldn't be overlooked if safety is a priority.

One of the best ways to stay safe is to use good judgment before attempting to ski a given slope. If you think a hill might be too steep or dangerous for you to handle, it's best to avoid it entirely. If you do find yourself in a dangerous situation, using techniques like sidestepping, sideslipping, or traversals to find safer slopes can help you avoid taking unnecessary risks.

An understanding of how trail rating systems and ski lifts work should help you when planning a safe route. There are also ideal safety practices to consider, such as riding with others or using communication devices. Using all of the tools and knowledge available is extremely beneficial for people who are serious about navigating the mountain safely.

10 EQUIPMENT MAINTENANCE

If you have your own gear and want to keep it functional year after year, it might be beneficial to read these maintenance tips. Some simple maintenance helps keep your equipment in peak performance. Gear maintenance takes just a little time or consideration, and simply drying out your equipment after use prevents a majority of issues from developing (such as molding, rusting, and other forms of deterioration).

Before attempting to do maintenance on your skis, it might be a good idea to watch a tutorial video online to help guide you through the process. Having a visual reference can be helpful, as some of the following maintenance tips can potentially damage your equipment if not done properly. While general maintenance is often easy and simple, some maintenance requires some extra attention and familiarity with specialized tools.

GENERAL MAINTENANCE

The vast majority of your ski gear just needs to be dried after use, which will keep ski equipment in great shape for a long time. Your ski boots, ski gloves, ski jacket, ski pants, ski goggles, helmet, poles, and skis should be stored somewhere dry and warm after use. The importance of this is fairly self-explanatory, as wet gear can deteriorate quickly in various ways (molding, rusting, etc.).

Beyond that, you may eventually need to reapply waterproofing treatments to your gloves, jacket, and pants. Leather gloves, for example, require an occasional leather treatment to keep them waterproof. A separate waterproofing treatment may be needed for your other pieces of equipment, and the type of waterproofing treatment will depend on the type of fabric being treated. Make sure you're using highly rated waterproofing products if you ever need to revive your equipment, and be aware that machine washing or machine drying your gear can reduce their waterproofing capabilities.

Ski Maintenance (Overview and Required Tools)

The most time-consuming piece of equipment to maintain are the skis. Aside from properly drying and storing your skis after use, maintaining your skis requires some additional attention using various specialized tools. To maintain your skis, you'll need a scraping tool that won't damage the base, a flat-iron (or a similar tool for melting and distributing wax), a filing tool to sharpen or detune your edges, and some ski wax. There are also a variety of repair kits or materials available to fix specific issues, such as filling deep gouges or re-sealing delaminating edges.

Maintaining your skis can be broken down to three steps. The first step is renewing edge sharpness, which requires a filing tool. The second step is maintaining a healthy base, which requires you to apply wax to the bottom of your skis regularly. The last step is remedying imperfections on your ski, which would only appear after they've become significantly damaged.

Ski Edge Maintenance

When it comes to ski maintenance, it's a good idea to start with the edges because they are relatively easy to care for. The edges of your skis should be sharpened to a 90° angle, with no rust or divots. A simple filing tool is all you need to renew your ski's edges, ensuring they carve into snow or ice as efficiently as possible. Be wary that the ski's edges can easily cut through skin when properly sharpened, and even dull skis should be handled with care.

When sharpening your edges, be very careful not to cut yourself. If you run your finger (carefully and safely) along the edges of your skis, you should be able to identify any areas that need sharpening. It might be a good idea to wear thick protective gloves for this, as they'll help prevent cuts and you should still be able to tell if the edges are uniformly sharp. Areas that are rusty, dull sections, or sections that feel jagged will need to be sharpened.

Sometimes you can see these issues visually, but the touch method is a reliable way to identify any issues. If you don't notice any of these imperfections, then your edges are fine and no maintenance is needed.

If you notice any flaws on your ski's edges, take a fine flat file tool and run it along the bottom of your metal edges. Sharpening your bottom edges will require the file to be parallel and flush with the base, but be careful not to scratch your ski's base. It shouldn't take much effort to knock the burrs flat. You should work with the filing tool to flow along the edges, as opposed to forcing the file to power through it. Long, smooth strokes are more effective when filing edges. You can make multiple passes if needed, but avoid removing too much metal. This should be a relatively quick process that only requires a few passes with the filing tool.

Once you finish the bottom portion of the edges (the part that is flat with your ski's base), move onto the side edges of the ski. Keep your file perpendicular to the ski's base, so that you are filing the same angle that the side edges are positioned. You should notice that the ski's metal edges form a roughly 90° corner around the sides of the ski, and you'll need to match this angle when filing the side edges of a ski.

Don't over-sharpen your metal edges. There's only so much metal that you can afford to shave off. If you're spending a lot of time sharpening, then you might be taking too much metal off your ski. You'll know your sharpening work is done when your edges feel sharp and are angled to 90-degrees. There should be no excessive burrs, jagged areas, rough patches, or rusty patches when you're finished. Once again, be very careful not to cut yourself when handling your ski's edges. Although the edges of a ski are not as pronounced as a knife's edge, the sharpened edge of a ski can cut into skin as easily as a blade would.

Alternatively, you can detune your ski's edges by rounding the ski's edges with a filing tool instead of sharpening them. This would only be recommended if you are primarily using your skis to grind boxes and rails. If you choose to detune your skis, then you'll likely never manage to rebuild a 90° edge. Once the metal edge of your ski is removed, it is not easily recovered. The process for detuning your skis is self-explanatory, simply angle or round your metal edges using a filing tool. Many people will keep certain sections of their skis sharp, such as the leading edges towards the nose, while detuning the sections of the skis that will be in contact with a rail while grinding. It's not something I would recommend for a beginner or intermediate-level skier, but certain skiers will find detuning useful for their skiing goals.

WAXING YOUR SKIS

Waxing your skis is an important part of regular ski maintenance, as wax prevents the base of the skis from drying out and performing poorly. A fresh coat of wax is needed whenever you encounter "sticky" snow while skiing. "Sticky" snow is a sudden slowdown issue that feels uncomfortable or jarring, like a ghost randomly grabbing your skis and trying to throw you off balance. You can also tell when your skis need wax if your base appears dusty or flakey. Wax is only applied to the bottoms of your skis, and you'll never need to apply wax to the topsheets or sides of your skis. There are two types of waxes: hot waxes and cold waxes. Hot waxes need to be melted onto your skis, whereas cold waxes or "rub-on" waxes can simply be applied by hand. Keep in mind that some ski waxes are made with questionable chemicals, such as PFAS or other hazardous compounds. Since you'll be handling ski wax fairly frequently as a skier, it's worth choosing a product that uses harmless ingredients.

While hot waxing is typically seen as the more reliable and long-term approach to waxing, it's possible to make mistakes that could damage your skis when applying it. Follow instructions carefully to ensure you're waxing properly. It might be helpful to follow a video tutorial for a visual reference before attempting to wax your own skis. Rub-on wax is a good wax choice for skiers who think they might damage their skis, but keep in mind that regularly applying hot wax will do a better job of protecting your ski's base over time. Additionally, most ski shops offer hot waxing services at a reasonable price.

Whichever type of wax you prefer to use, you'll need a scraping tool to remove all the old wax from the bottom of your skis before applying a fresh coat. Be sure to use a scraping tool that doesn't damage your base. I recommend using a scraping tool specially designed for skis, but you could use any scraping tool as long as it doesn't scratch or gouge your skis.

Rub-on wax is a self-explanatory type of wax. You essentially just rub this type of wax directly on your skis by hand. You can make multiple passes until you have an even coat of wax. It might take some effort to transfer rub-on wax onto the skis. Rub-on wax can be especially useful when you are experiencing issues on the mountain, as it can be applied quickly throughout the day. You may need to scrape the old wax off your skis before reapplying rub-on wax, however, since rub-on wax is removed while skiing I've found this is often an unnecessary step.

Technically, you can apply hot waxes directly to your skis like they are rub-on waxes. That being said, cold waxes are softer than hard waxes so that they can be applied easily. You'd need to use an impressive level of strength to apply hot waxes by rubbing them directly onto your skis, so pay attention to the labeling when choosing the wax that's right for you.

Hot waxes (sometimes called hard waxes) are longer-lasting ski waxes, which can be more convenient when skiing multiple days in a row. Applying hot wax requires a heating tool, such as a hot iron, to melt and distribute the wax. Hard waxes offer increased performance and reliability, which is why most experienced skiers prefer to apply this type of wax to their skis.

Keep in mind that using a hot iron to wax your skis will render the iron useless for ironing clothes, as the residual wax will ruin clothing. You might need to tie your ski brakes up to get them out of the way for the next steps. The ski brakes are located on the heel portion of the ski binding. If you're new to hot waxing you should look up a video tutorial detailing this process, as a visual reference can help skiers avoid damaging their skis.

Before you apply hot wax to your skis, you need to remove the previous layers of wax with a scraping tool. There may not be much wax on your base by the time it needs waxing, so this shouldn't take more than a few minutes. You'll know you're done scraping wax if you cannot easily remove any wax from the bottom of your skis. When you're finished, wipe down your skis so that no dust or wax flakes are visible on the base. After ensuring the bottoms of your skis are clean, preheat your flat iron in preparation for the next step.

To effectively apply hot wax without damaging a pair of skis you'll need to iron quickly, as prolonged contact will cause your ski's base to burn or bubble. It's a good idea to start at the lowest temperature settings possible, slowly turning up the heat until the iron can easily melt the ski wax. You can potentially ruin a good pair of skis if your iron's temperature settings are too high, but you also don't want your temperature settings low enough that your iron struggles to melt the wax. As long as you keep these things in mind, you should have little trouble finding the ideal temperature settings. Some irons have precise temperature settings, in which case you can match the heat settings to the ideal melting temperature listed on your wax brand's application instructions.

Test the iron by rubbing your brick of hard wax directly on the hot plate, and slowly increase the temperature if it doesn't easily melt. If you notice any smoke coming off the iron, it could be a sign that your temperature settings are too high. The wax should steadily melt until it drips onto the bottom of your skis and forms a puddle. When you have a decent amount of wax pooled, you can begin to spread the wax by running the hot iron lengthwise until the ski is coated. Don't worry if the wax stops spreading easily, just melt some more puddles of wax as needed.

You may notice that the wax hardens quickly once it pools onto the ski. For this reason, it's a good idea to work quickly. It's also important to make multiple passes instead of focusing the iron's heat on one section for too long. You should notice that the wax is melting and spreading after a few quick passes. Let the skis cool down between passes or make a new puddle of wax to avoid potential damage.

If you're still having trouble distributing the wax, there are two likely causes. The first issue might be that you're ironing too quickly, in which case you should first try slowing down your ironing speeds. If you're ironing the same spots repeatedly and the wax isn't melting or spreading, the iron might need to be slightly hotter. Once you have distributed an even coat of wax on both skis, allow the wax to cool and move onto the final step.

The final step is to remove the excess wax with a scraping tool. While this step seems like a waste of wax, removing the excess wax provides the best performance on the snow. Don't worry, your skis will still have a protective layer of wax after this final scraping. Be careful not to scrape too excessively though, as a light scraping should be sufficient. You'll know you're finished when you've removed the clumps of wax and there is a slight shine on the base. You can also finish off your waxing job by lightly buffing your ski's base with a soft scuff pad and making a lengthwise sweep with a base brush, but this is an optional step that doesn't significantly enhance the end result.

After a fresh waxing, you'll notice a significant boost in speed and your skis will glide effortlessly on the snow. The waxing process may sound complicated at first, but it becomes quite simple once you get the hang of it. While it can be a tedious process, waxing is an important part of ski maintenance that keeps your bases in great condition.

FIXING GOUGES

While small scratches can be covered with a layer of wax, deep gouges will require some special care. Fixing gouges is a fairly straightforward process, but you'll need a ski repair kit to ensure you have all the required materials. When choosing a ski repair kit, make sure that the filler material matches your ski's base. Dark ski bases use a black filler material, while light or colored ski bases use a transparent gouge filler.

To begin fixing a gouged ski base, use a knife to cut away the jagged areas surrounding the gouge until the perimeter is smooth and below the rest of the pit. Repair kits use a material called P-Tex (a type of polyethylene) to fill gouges on the base. Ignite the P-Tex like a candle until it is melting and flowing uniformly, then pool the P-Tex over the gouged area until it completely fills the hole. Allow some time for the material to cool before using a razor to cut the excess P-Tex down. Next, use a filing tool to continue flattening the patched area. A scraping tool can be utilized to shave the rest completely flat, as long as most of the P-Tex has been removed. After applying a fresh layer of hot wax over the patched area, the repair should be complete and permanent.

REMEDYING DELAMINATION

Skis are typically made by layering various materials that are glued together (generally with epoxy resin). The separation of a ski's layers is what's known as delamination. Over time and repeated use, your ski's inner layers might start to separate. You can easily diagnose ski delamination when the areas of separation start to become visible. When skis begin to delaminate, water seeps into the inner layers and slowly worsens the issue.

Luckily, you can fix this with a clamp and some epoxy resin (or superglue). Make sure that the bonding agent you're using is effective for the materials you're gluing together, and ensure that your skis are dry before you start to fix the delaminated areas. After that, simply add a couple drops of superglue to the gaps before clamping the delaminated area flush with the rest of the ski. This should reseal the ski and keep water and ice from making the issue worse. Make sure you don't get any glue on your base. It's also a good idea to use cardboard or a similar buffer to prevent the clamp from damaging your ski.

Some skis may develop issues that are unrepairable, but these maintenance tips should help keep your gear in peak performance year after year. Simply drying your gear and properly storing equipment will go a long way in ensuring your equipment stays in great shape. Some additional maintenance, such as waxing and tuning your ski's edges, will also help keep your equipment in excellent condition. Many ski resorts, equipment rental companies, and gear shops also offer ski maintenance services. This can be a good option for people who aren't great with tools or don't have the time to maintain their own gear.

11 NOT DYING

Skiing can be a dangerous sport, with unique hazards that most people aren't knowledgeable about. To make matters worse, crashing on skis is an inevitability. If you do happen to get into trouble, there are some things you can do to minimize the chances of injury or death. Luckily, your chances of getting seriously injured while skiing are fairly low. The chances of dying while skiing are even lower. Still, it's worth knowing about the risks so that you can prepare for them or avoid them entirely.

SLIDING

While sliding is a potentially dangerous situation when you lose control, there are some advantages to sliding in a crash. Sliding reduces the initial impact forces you experience when falling, which is why landing jumps on a downhill incline is less impactful than landing jumps on flat ground. If you feel that you are falling (and if there are no trees or rocks directly downhill from you) it can be worth positioning yourself for a slide instead of bracing for impact. Wrist injuries are common in the sport due to people's natural reaction to use their hands to catch themselves after a fall. However, the speeds a skier experiences are too great for this strategy to be effective. It's often better to position your body so that you can slide with the hill feet first, using the edges of your skis to halt forward progress.

Of course, an uncontrollable slide on steep terrain is one of the most dangerous positions you can find yourself in as a skier. If you find yourself in an uncontrolled slide, you should squat or curl into a ball immediately. Curling up or squatting down gives a person the ability to extend their legs into the snow, which helps them engage the edges of their skis or ski boots. Using your edges in this way is the only way to effectively stop during an uncontrolled slide, especially when sliding on ice. If you are tumbling and curling up makes the situation worse, you could "starfish" your body by extending your limbs in an attempt to slow rotations. Once you have slowed the rotations of your crash you can try curling or squatting again, which will ideally put you in position to engage your edges and slow down.

HARSH WEATHER, FROSTBITE, AND HYPOTHERMIA

We talked about snow conditions earlier, however, we didn't go in detail on the specific dangers they present. Blizzards, high winds, and whiteouts are some examples of weather conditions that could quickly become dangerous for skiers. The cold weather a skier experiences can also increase the chances of developing conditions such as frostbite or hypothermia

Visibility is one concern in **harsh weather conditions,** as vision can become restricted in certain weather. Blizzards, whiteouts, and other weather conditions can obscure visibility, sometimes to the point where it's too dangerous to ski. If you're having trouble seeing due to the weather, you may have to ski slower or practice on safer terrain than you normally would.

Exposure to this type of weather is also a concern. While things like frostbite and hypothermia are rare, they are medical conditions you should be knowledgeable about in cold environments. Exposed skin cools rapidly in high winds or when wet, which is why ski jackets, snow pants, and snow gloves are designed to be windproof and waterproof. It's also why I recommend choosing snow clothes that are also insulated.

Hypothermia begins to set in when a person's core body temperature drops below 95°F (35°C), and becomes a severe or life threatening condition at temperatures below 89 to 90°F (32°C). People usually know when they are developing hypothermia because they'll be extremely cold long before the symptoms of hypothermia are present. Generally speaking, people will do whatever they can to avoid this discomfort. The earliest warning sign that someone is developing hypothermia is excessive shivering. The more serious warning signs are confusion, stiff muscles, slow breathing, sleepiness, and difficulty coordinating movement. The final and most dangerous stage of hypothermia is a weak pulse, followed by a nonexistent pulse. The only way to prevent hypothermia from reaching these final stages is to warm the core body temperature, which is why specialized snow clothing is essential for skiers.

If you think you are beginning to develop hypothermia, there are a few things you can do. Find shelter first, then remove wet clothing and do your best to warm up. In a survival scenario, warming up might require making a fire or huddling with other people for warmth. In an emergency you can't be shy, people have recovered from hypothermia using skin-to-skin contact. You can interpret that information however you like!

Frostbite is a condition where the skin and living cells just below the skin are destroyed after freezing. The more common type of damage is frostnip, where your skin recovers after warming up. Frostnip goes away after a few days of tenderness, leading to flaking skin that eventually heals. Frostbite is more severe and could lead to complications without medical attention. Because of how uncomfortable skin gets in harsh environments, these are somewhat rare and can be prevented by protecting exposed skin (for example with ear muffs, balaclavas, scarves, beanies, etc.).

While frostnip and frostbite are rare, the danger comes when your skin stops feeling uncomfortable and starts feeling numb. At this point, long periods of exposure can go unnoticed due to the lack of any pain or feeling in the area. If your skin starts turning white, or God forbid purple, you're beginning to experience the late stages of frostbite and might need assistance from a medical professional in order to heal.

I actually experienced frostnip for the first time while writing this book, and the only reason I developed this condition is because I ignored the uncomfortable warning signs my exposed skin was giving me. The pain I was feeling went away once my skin was completely numb, which could have been avoided if I was being honest about what my body was trying to tell me. Needless to say, I wasn't protecting myself enough to stay comfortable. Fortunately, the damage to my skin only resulted with a minor blister that healed quickly.

The moral of the story is that you have to be prepared for the conditions you might face as a skier. You also have to recognize when the risks are too great. Whether that's from being too cold or from changing weather conditions that makes skiing more difficult, being rational about the situation at hand will go a long way towards keeping you safe.

NATURAL HAZARDS

Half-buried trees, exposed rocks, cliffs, streams, and sinkholes are some examples of natural hazards that can endanger a rider. Ski patrol will section these hazards off at most ski resorts, but regardless of where you're skiing you should always be scanning your environment for potential hazards.

One of the best strategies to identify natural hazards is to use the buddy system to scout ahead, spot obstacles, and keep each other safe if there's ever an accident. Working together with other riders is a great way to avoid otherwise unforeseen obstacles. The buddy system is one of the few ways to identify **cliffs or similar drop hazards**. Skiing with a group can also be a lifeline in worst-case scenarios, leading to faster rescue if something were to happen.

Half-buried trees are obstacles that are usually easy to spot. The real danger that trees pose are the hazardous phenomena known as "**tree wells**." When a tree blocks a wide enough radius of falling snow with their branches, it creates a hollow void that surrounds the trunk called a tree well. Not all trees will form tree wells, which can lead to skiers developing a false sense of security when riding near trees. Tree wells are deceptive, as the pocket surrounding a tree can suddenly give way and catch a rider by surprise. Riding too close to one can collapse the void, so give the trees some room and respect. If you are unfortunate enough to fall into one, try not to struggle initially. Excess movement can pull more snow down on top of you, further complicating the situation. Instead, you should find a way to call for help or signal to other riders for rescue. Try to keep your head up above the snow and grab onto anything solid that you can. If you're curious about tree wells and want to learn more, check out the pinned video on my TikTok account (*@mchenrybooks*) to see how I escaped from a tree well while snowboarding. Ski areas with high geothermal activity can also create similar hollow pockets under the snow, which can be even harder to anticipate. Yet another reason why riding in groups is so important.

Rooftops and similar overhanging structures accumulate snow and form icicles throughout the year. In the United States alone, icicles kill around fifteen people a year. These frozen spears are dangerous, so don't spend time standing underneath rooftops or overhanging structures if you can avoid it. Rooftops also shed snow periodically, especially when temperatures are warmer and snow begins to melt. A rooftop shedding snow is like a miniature avalanche, and you don't want to be caught underneath one. As a general rule, you should look up before passing underneath an overhang and avoid lingering near structures that could shed snow or icicles.

Snowmelt can form **streams or rivers that flow underneath the snow**. If you find yourself in a natural channel on the mountain, it might be worth seeking the high ground to avoid these potential water hazards underneath the snow. If you hear running water, you should be extremely cautious and stay away from lower sections of the slope where fall lines meet. In other words, stay as high on the slope as possible when conditions are warm enough to melt snow.

Natural hazards are some of the greatest dangers a skier can encounter, but luckily most skiers will be able to identify and avoid them. Using the buddy system is one of the best strategies to maintain awareness and avoid natural hazards. Riding in terrain suitable for your current skill level is another great way to avoid losing control. When it comes to natural hazards, a little knowledge on the topic goes a long way.

AVALANCHES (NOT AS COMMON AS YOU MIGHT THINK)

The overwhelming majority of avalanches are small or inconsequential. For most skiers, especially beginner or intermediate-level skiers, avalanches are rare and practically harmless. In populated areas like ski towns and ski resorts, snow conditions are carefully monitored and controlled to prevent the formation of large avalanches. Places that are at risk for developing large avalanches will task avalanche specialists to frequently trigger small avalanches, which reduces the chances that a large one can build up and become more dangerous. That being said, it's worth knowing how to spot avalanches before they occur.

When it snows, layers are deposited in what's known as "slabs." Often, these slabs of snow have slightly different qualities. For example, the snow conditions might form a light and fluffy slab one day, followed by a heavy slab composed of wet snow the next. If a fluffy snow slab forms underneath a slab of heavy snow, it could suddenly collapse and cause a sudden shift. This sudden shift is usually caused by skiers or other riders, although they can sometimes be triggered on their own.

When a snow layer suddenly shifts, a wave of snow begins to slide down the mountain. In this respect, an avalanche behaves similarly to a mudslide or a landslide. The amount of snow that shifts can be large or very small, but it's the large avalanches that concern most people. A significant amount of snow, combined with a very steep slope, is needed to trigger an avalanche with destructive or dangerous potential.

Since most avalanches are triggered by people, skiers who attempt to ride in steep terrain should be extra cautious while actively looking for signs of danger. Certain terrain is more likely to develop the conditions that could lead to an avalanche. Some of the terrain factors that increase the odds of an avalanche are low ground cover, steep slopes, convex-shaped slopes, and the wind direction. Ground cover refers to things like trees or large rocks, which helps the snowfall pack down and cling to the mountain. Steep and convex-shaped (meaning rounded or bubble-shaped) hills are sloped in a way that encourages snow to slide, instead of compacting down as snow does on flatter surfaces. The direction the wind blows can also make a factor. For example, wind coming from the north of a hill will blow snow to the south, forming a snow layer with a different consistency on the southern side of the hill. Other factors to look for that raise the chances of an avalanche are recent storms, a high rate of snowfall, changing temperatures, and wet snow.

One of the telltale signs that an avalanche is inevitable is when sudden cracks appear in the snow. The formation of cracks in the snow indicate movement, meaning a slab of snow could be shifting. There are also snow features that can collapse quickly, such as exposed slabs of overhanging snow. These snow features are called cornices, and if they shift or break they can trigger an avalanche. Pinwheels are another telltale sign of increased avalanche danger. Pinwheels somewhat resemble large snail shells, and they indicate that the snow is starting to lose hold and becoming more inclined to sliding downhill.

If you see sudden cracks in the snow or suspect an avalanche may occur, try to ski higher than the trigger points. Cracks in the snow indicate that everything downhill from the fault line (not to be confused with the fall line) is at risk of sliding downhill. If you can ski higher than the cracks in the snow, you might be able to avoid the avalanche entirely.

Although avalanches are rare, they are extremely dangerous if you become trapped in one. Knowing what to do in these situations could save your life. If you are caught by the sliding snow, make swimming motions to stay on the surface. If you can, try to aim for the side of the avalanche. Before coming to a stop, get your hands in front of your face and form a pocket of air in the snow. If you see someone caught in the avalanche, mark the last place you saw them with a pole and probe the snow downhill from that point with your other pole. Only get help if it is very close, as most people can't survive under the snow for longer than an hour. You'll have the best chance of finding trapped victims if you look for signs of movement under the snow, listen closely for any muffled yells, and methodically sweep the path of the avalanche. The most important thing to do after an avalanche is to stay calm. Staying calm makes rescue efforts more effective and extends survival time for trapped individuals.

If you believe that the avalanche risk is high in your location, there are some additional life-saving tools that you should consider carrying. Avalanche beacons are devices that can guide rescuers to your location using radio frequencies, and they are commonly used by ski patrol and experienced skiers to locate individuals buried in snow. Compact shovels are another recommended tool, as they are lightweight and fit neatly in a backpack. Shovels can be used to rescue people trapped in the snow, in addition to having other uses like building shelter in a survival situation. Avalanche airbags are another recent invention that can be manually deployed to reduce the chances of becoming completely buried. All of these strategies require skiers to ride in groups, increasing the odds of a speedy rescue in a worst-case scenario.

While it is a good idea to be knowledgeable about avalanches, the chances of a beginner or intermediate-level skier encountering one at a ski resort is practically zero. Even in expert terrain, it takes very specific conditions to trigger an avalanche that is potentially dangerous. That being said, there's no harm in educating yourself about the signs and conditions that lead to potential avalanches.

WILDLIFE

As odd as it may sound, you should be aware that wildlife encounters can occur on the mountain. Snowy mountain climates are notoriously hostile and unforgiving environments, so it's unbelievably rare to encounter animals that could potentially pose a danger to humans while skiing. Although rare, there are a few dangerous critters that you might see while skiing.

Mountain goats, elk, and moose can be extremely hostile if approached. These herbivores can be territorial, moody, and are incredibly strong animals. While it might be tempting to get a closer look at these majestic beasts, they have been known to injure or kill a surprising amount of people. As prey animals, they are used to defending themselves from potential predators. They will also commonly fight amongst their own species. Moose and goats are especially dangerous animals, so it's best to admire these creatures from afar.

There are also a few predators that can inhabit the mountains. Bears will mostly hibernate during these winter months, but it's still possible to spot one during their hibernation period (usually if their dens become damaged or flooded). Like most wildlife, they will try their best to avoid humans. That said, they can be potentially aggressive if you surprise one.

Depending on your location, big cats such as mountain lions or bobcats may be present. Wild cats have been known to travel vast distances in the search for food, and are highly territorial when it comes to other cats. They have exceptional vision and hearing, however, they are pretty good at using that hearing and vision to actively avoid humans. The chance of encountering a big cat while skiing is practically zero. Even if you were to see one, they are opportunistic hunters that are often scared of humans. While they are incredibly rare to see and generally avoid humans, they are also potentially dangerous. For reference, mountain goats are roughly 600% more likely to attack humans than a mountain lion. Bobcats have never been documented attacking humans, and lynx will generally not attack people.

Spotting any of these animals while skiing is an overwhelmingly rare occurrence, and if you give these animals the respect they deserve they will likely not bother you. Still, it might be worth educating yourself about the wildlife in your location.

As long as you're being honest with your skill level and abilities, there's nothing out there that's worth fearing as a skier. Yet you should not go into this sport blindly either. Be knowledgeable about the potential hazards. Maintain control of your skis at all times by riding terrain you are comfortable with. Be aware of your surroundings. Prepare for the environment. And above all, have fun with it.

If I've taught you nothing else, remember to ski with a friend. Using the buddy system is a great way to increase awareness, expedite learning, and facilitate faster rescues if accidents occur.

12 WRAPPING UP

Skiing is a dynamic sport, and one that is a lot of fun. There's nothing quite as exhilarating as the feeling of skiing freely down the mountain, or landing a cool new trick that you've been practicing. Your progression in skiing is a journey. Growth in this sport doesn't happen overnight, and that's what makes the journey more rewarding. As long as you are having fun with the sport, your story will be a story of success.

This book serves as a comprehensive guide to skiing, so that you can safely embark on that adventure and enjoy it to the fullest. The best way to have fun is to stay out of harm's way, which is why I emphasize the importance of safety while you're learning how to ski. The lessons provided serve to keep you protected while mastering the skills needed to succeed, contributing to your feelings of comfort and joy.

If I've done my job correctly, then dying should be the least of your worries. All it takes to ski safely is to be prepared for the elements, knowledgeable about the potential hazards, and to practice on hills within your ability level. Once you know how to control your skis, the likelihood of becoming a statistic is very small.

Since I've written at length detailing how to ski safely, one piece of advice I have is to emphasize the importance of having fun on your journey. What is the part about skiing that you most enjoy? Is it sharing this unique experience with your friends? Is it the time you get to spend with your family? Is it the feeling you experience while skiing? Is it the beautiful views, or the smell of the crisp mountain air? Is it the sense of community on the mountain? Whatever it is, focus on those aspects and maximize your time having fun on the snow. "Getting good" certainly has its rewards, but having fun is the name of the game. Your level of joy is more important than your level of expertise.

My final message goes out to the parents.
Remember to go easy on the kids. I see garbage parents out
there yelling at their kids every day. You don't want to be
that person. You know the ones, the people yelling at their
children on the mountain. An adult intent on breaking kids
down instead of building them up. The reason I stuck with
this sport, and reached the ability level I have today, is that
my teachers had patience. My dad and my grandpa let me
figure things out on my own time, and they stuck by my
side when I was just learning how to ski. As I got older and
started outskiing them, I started having to wait. While my
grandpa passed too soon, I will always stick by my dad's
side when we ski (regardless of how good the snow is that
day). If you want that type of experience when you grow
old, it starts with the example you set for the children.

Thanks for choosing me to teach these lessons, and
I hope that you've found the information I've provided
useful. The support I get from readers is my inspiration to
write, and I hope you'll continue to support my publishing
efforts in the future. For now, I'm probably done writing

sports guides. I'm currently working on my first fiction novels, but I won't bore you with those details. Check out my social media links if you're interested in my creative endeavors and want to stay updated!

Good luck out there, have fun, and don't die!

ABOUT THE AUTHOR

Kyle grew up on the Olympic Peninsula near the edge of the Olympic National Park. He was taught how to ski by his dad and his grandpa at a young age, primarily at the Hurricane Ridge and Alpine Meadows ski areas. With his grandpa's experience as an adaptive ski instructor and a member of ski patrol, he quickly became an expert skier. He later started teaching the next generation of skiers and snowboarders through lessons offered at Snoqualmie Pass, and he continues to educate riders through private lessons and his publishing efforts.

Kyle graduated from Washington State University with a Bachelor's Degree in Sport Science. Although he originally intended to pursue a career in physical therapy, he experienced several setbacks and decided to take a chance with his writing instead. After the success of his first book *How to Snowboard (Have Fun) and Not Die,* he has since published several books across multiple genres.

As an avid skier and snowboarder, he is especially fond of exploring the backcountry in search of unique natural features to ride. While he began his writing career publishing snowboard

214

guides under the pen name of "Kyle Ashton," he recently began publishing more creative works under the pen name "M.C. Henry." If you would like to support his efforts, feel free to follow him on TikTok or Instagram at *@mchenrybooks*. You can also reach out to him directly via social media for inquiries.

Kyle recently achieved his dream of buying a mountain home and is eagerly awaiting the birth of his first child in February. He continues to share his love of skiing and snowboarding with close friends and family. Kyle plans to publish his first horror novel in 2024, which is a goal that he has been diligently working on for some time now. He also had his first podcast appearance this year, and is looking forward to similar opportunities in the future.

If you found this guide to skiing useful, be sure to leave a review or recommend a copy to a friend. It's a nice gesture, helps support his work, and he appreciates the feedback!

Printed in Great Britain
by Amazon

37312945R00126